THE POWER OF
THE THIRD RAIL

THE POWER OF THE THIRD RAIL

A Testimony of Life and Hope in Suffering and Ministry

Jim Shaw MD

To order additional copies of this book, contact:
Xlibris
1-888-795-4274
www.Xlibris.com
Orders@Xlibris.com
764623

CONTENTS

Contents

NEWS OF THE FIRE AHEAD

**"When you walk through the fire
you will not be burned."** ~ Isa. 43:2b

"We have a problem here. We have a real problem here . . ."

These were the words I heard from the radiologist as he met me coming out of the MRI scanner at Riverside Hospital on July 12, 1997.

Although I had been having neck pain for several months, my wife and I had been working on our plans for a medical Missions trip to Zimbabwe with Medical Missions International. However, as the pain was progressively getting worse, I began thinking that I had a ruptured disc or a bad arthritic neck, so I called one of my neurosurgeon friends and he ordered an MRI scan.

However when I came out of the scanner, what the radiologist showed me as he put the films up on the light box, almost caused me to faint. My knees weakened and my heart knotted up into my throat. There on the film was a large tumor that had replaced half of the vertebral body at the base of my neck. This tumor was growing out of the bone into the adjacent soft tissue—a very ugly picture if you are a doctor and know something about what you are viewing.

My first thought was, "You're a dead man, Shaw."

This is my testimony of how God used His Power to connect and bless the two tracks in my life over the last eighteen years—our development of the Lackey Free Clinic, a ministry to indigent, uninsured residents of the Virginia Peninsula and my battle with multiple myeloma, a bone marrow cancer,

PREFACE

"Each one should use whatever gift he has received to serve others, faithfully administering God's grace." ~ 1 Pet. 4:10

Growing up in Richmond, Virginia, I was surrounded by family. My grandmother, several aunts, and an uncle lived on both sides of our house. The eldest of two sons, I had an idyllic childhood; my parents and younger brother were loving and I was blessed with good health, high academic performance, and athletic abilities that allowed me to excel in high school football and track.

I met Cooka, a beautiful girl with blond hair, at a sleigh riding party when I was in the eighth grade. I was smitten— I think it was love at first sight. We dated throughout high school and especially enjoyed spending summer weekends together at her family's house on the Rappahannock River, where fishing, waterskiing and smooching were favorite activities. As seniors in 1962, I was co-captain of the football team and she was a homecoming queen and cheerleader, a person of buoyant spirit- a trait that would become essential to our surviving the health storms that were to come.

After our high school graduation, Cooka began nursing school in Richmond, and I enrolled in a pre-med curriculum at Randolph-Macon College in Ashland, Virginia; a mere thirty minutes from the nursing school. I was so in love that I could not imagine attending a college farther away from her. I was also hoping to play college football and had a better chance of being able to play at a small school like Randolph-Macon than at a larger university.

We were married after her graduation from nursing school when she had gotten a job at a local hospital. She could now support us during my med school years. We exchanged vows on July 10, one of the hottest days of 1965.

We spent my senior year of college living in an off campus shack—an old, porous, and poorly insulated rental house with an oil circulator furnace that only heated two out of the four rooms. It was a time for memories to be made. Most winter nights, she had to prepare dinner in an unheated kitchen, wearing a heavy winter coat and wool hat! Still, to her it was a castle, and we were happy to be together in a place we called our home.

Following college, I attended medical school at the Medical College of Virginia (MCV; now the Virginia Commonwealth University). It was an exciting and enriching time for me—I was able to live out my passion to be a doctor, while digesting the myriad of facts and facets of medical science.

In July 1969, the summer of my last year of medical school, we were blessed by the birth of our son, Travis. Our little family had begun to grow.

I had set a personal goal of obtaining the best training possible to become a pulmonary physician. Securing that training meant moving out of Richmond and away from the family and friends with whom we had spent the last twenty-six years of our lives. This was a daunting and sad prospect, particularly for Cooka, who was by then pregnant with our second child and wanted desperately to have the support of our families.

We had reservations and anxieties about the separation, but I felt sure that I had to put my training and career above family at that time. With the benefit of hindsight, I can now see that this was not the best choice. Looking back on what has transpired in my professional career, I now believe that I could have stayed in Virginia and honored my wife's wishes without damaging my career. There are still times when I wrestle with regret over this decision—I would have liked my children to have enjoyed the benefits of growing up with their grandparents close by.

We continued moving over the next twelve years for various training and medical school faculty positions. Our first stop was New Haven, Connecticut at Yale University for an Internal Medicine Residency.

Our daughter, Ashley, was born three weeks following this move, delivered by an obstetrician that Cooka had never met. I was working every second or third night, so we were grateful my mom was able to come and stay with us for the first two weeks following delivery, to not only help my wife recover but to help care for a one-year-old and a newborn. Remember, there was no paternity leave in the 1970s.

This was a difficult time, perhaps the worst year of our married life. Cooka felt abandoned in a strange city with two small children. I was working such long hours that I wasn't able to stay awake even when I was home. Looking back on that time now, we definitely believe that God's hand was protecting us. We were determined that nothing was going to break up our marriage despite this highly stressful circumstance. And God worked through Cooka during this time, as she generously gave me gobs of grace during my times of sleep deprivation, irritability, and poor communication.

In 1973, we moved again, this time to San Diego. There, I spent four years of training in fellowships in Pulmonary Diseases and Immunopathology.

By 1977, I knew that I needed to seek real employment; there were two choices: either go into a pulmonary private practice or pursue a faculty job at a medical school. Because I had developed a keen interest in research, I accepted a position as Assistant Professor of Medicine at University of Texas San Antonio. In this position, I conducted lab research and taught pulmonary fellows and medical students.

Although we both loved Texas, we knew in our hearts that we ultimately wanted to return to Virginia. So, in 1982, we moved once again, when an opportunity arose for me to join a solo pulmonary practitioner in Newport News. It proved to be a wonderful move for our families—my parents now had easy access to us and to the two grandchildren who had been so far away for the previous twelve years.

Thankfully, throughout the next sixteen years, I was blessed by God with a busy and rewarding practice at Riverside Hospital. I was healthy and active and spent as much time as possible outdoors running, white water canoeing, rafting, hunting and fishing. Our family had always been healthy and active.

We were not prepared for the devastating news we would soon face.

God and a Model Train Track

"And surely I am with you always." ~ Matt. 28:20

Like many kids of an earlier era, when I was five I got a Lionel Train set for Christmas. I still have it, and it still runs. This train set has entertained three generations of Shaw children, including most recently, our three grandchildren.

The Lionel track has three rails. The wheels of the train's cars and engine ride on the two outside rails; the middle or third rail is the power source. If you don't have the electricity hooked up to the third rail, your little engine doesn't have power and your train doesn't go anywhere.

If we assign the left rail to the Lackey Free Clinic ministry and the right rail to my battle with bone marrow cancer, we have a visual example of how these two major events have tracked alongside each other for the past nineteen years of my life.

The third rail, just as it represents the power from the electricity to run the engine, represents the power of Jesus Christ as He has driven these two forces: the Clinic ministry and cancer survival.

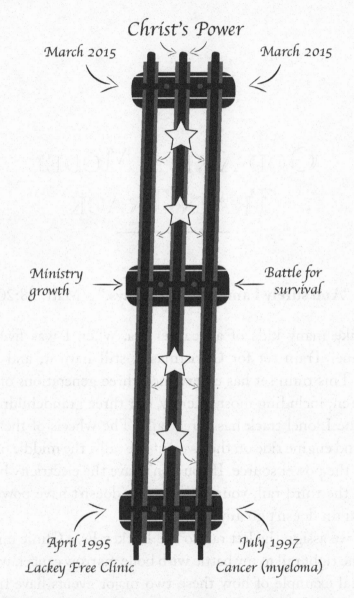

This is a graphic illustration of the Lionel model train track serving as a metaphor for Christ's Sovereignty. The third rail supplies the power (stars * with arrows → provides control for outer rails) for the Lackey Clinic ministry on the left rail, while supporting treatment and survival for multiple myeloma cancer on the right rail.

Jesus has been in the center of my life for twenty-two years. He has enabled me to connect the growth obtained from my suffering with multiple myeloma to the leadership needed to help Lackey Free Clinic expand from a tiny ministry with three volunteers only one night a week to one with 300 volunteers in a 10,000-square-foot facility, providing over 12,000 patient visits to indigent patients on the Virginia Peninsula.

Keep this train track analogy in your mind as I share with you how God used His Power to connect and bless these two tracks over the past nineteen years of my life.

This is my testimony of God's Providence at work in my life . . . a testimony of life and hope.

A Skeptic Finds Faith

―――――――――

"I still remember the day you saved me,
the day I heard you call out my name.
You said you loved me and would never leave
me, and I've never been the same." ~ Tommy
Walker, from "We Will Remember"

I was raised in the St. John's Episcopal Church in Richmond.
My earliest memories of church date from age five when I was
with the other kindergartners in Sunday school. At twelve,
I attended confirmation classes and was confirmed into the
congregation; I don't think I knew what this meant, except that
I was more of a "grown-up" and could now serve in the church.

After confirmation, I served as an acolyte nearly every
Sunday; lighting and extinguishing the altar candles, as well
as assisting the pastor with communion and other duties. This
gave me a real sense of reverence for God and His house, St.
John's. In this church there was never an altar call and I never
committed my life to Christ, but I think my belief in God was
real and I started praying on my own at bedtime.

―――

I don't remember understanding the Gospel; that Jesus died for my sins and I don't think the Gospel was ever preached—if it was, I did not hear it.

The one thing that has been forever etched in my mind from that time is that wonderful verse from John 14:6: "I am the Way, the Truth, and the Life," in large letters over the ceiling arch leading to the altar. I loved that verse then, but it means even more to me now, since understanding the second half of the verse ("No one comes to the Father, except through Me") when I came to Christ in 1993.

At about sixteen or seventeen, I became a crucifer, whose job is to carry the cross up high to lead the procession of the choir and pastor at the start and end of service.

I remember feeling awe and reverence for God during this time, but it was reserved for Sunday only, as faith, prayer and any Bible study was not lived out by anyone in my home on Monday through Saturday. However, I have cherished this time of my life at St. John's as I have grown in my relationship with Christ, and recognize that God planted a seed then; which, later in the spring of 1993, allowed the Holy Spirit to lead me to seek Him in His Word.

In college, I continued to attend church most Sundays with Cooka, and serve as a crucifer. In my sophomore year, all students at the Methodist Randolph Macon College were required to take Bible study for two semesters. I loved the Old Testament section which was taught first semester in Dr. T's course. I think this was because during my time at St. John's, the Bible was not necessarily emphasized and I hungered to know the Old Testament.

However, I came away from that Old Testament semester with the notion that supernatural events, such as the parting of the Red Sea, or the walls of Jericho falling down, were either myth or allegory and if they did occur it was by natural phenomena rather than the power of an omnipotent God. By second semester, when we got to the New Testament and the Gospel, I had turned off my mind to the Bible as truth.

Ironically, this course, no doubt designed and required in a Methodist college for young men to grow in faith, was a seminal event in destroying what shaky faith I had from my Episcopal upbringing.

We attended St. John's irregularly after my sophomore year. I think I went more out of a sense of duty to my parents than to a desire on my part.

After finishing medical school in 1970, we moved to New Haven, Connecticut, for three years, San Diego for four years for training, and then San Antonio for five years for a faculty position. During these times I was in my warrior phase, trying to become the best pulmonary doctor and researcher I could be. Cooka was trying to renew her roots in faith, trying out churches in each location. However, I was not supportive of her efforts to attend church, and in some instances I even opposed her trying to get our family out early on Sunday mornings.

This was a dark period for me spiritually, and this darkness covered Cooka's life as she regretfully gave up trying to bring God into our family.

The fallout was that our marriage went through several shaky periods. I brought home the job stresses of academic and private practice competition, without any foundation of faith in Jesus. It says in 1 Peter 5:8, "The devil prowls around like a roaring lion looking for someone to devour." I believe we were attacked by Satan at this time, as he blinded our minds as unbelievers, so that we could not see the light of the Gospel (2 Cor. 4:4).

In 1984, Cooka was invited by a good friend to the Christian Woman's Club meeting in Newport News. She felt drawn back to God and a few meetings later accepted Christ as her Lord and Savior following one of the testimonies given at the meeting. She started attending Community Bible Study (CBS) weekly and had an insatiable hunger for God's Word. She tried very hard to get me and the children interested in the Bible and going to church, but we all turned a deaf ear.

Cooka became direct in forcing her faith on us, especially me, and we argued frequently about my lack of interest. Only in recent years did I learn that she had shared with a Community Bible Study leader that she was planning to divorce me because she could not be a good Christian woman married to such a blatant non-believer. Thankfully, the leader convinced her that this was a poor decision and that she should remain in our marriage and pray for Christ to touch me.

Eventually, I gave in to attending Warwick Memorial Methodist Church in Newport News regularly with Cooka, mostly to please her. I personally had no interest in the Gospel, and most of the time fidgeted throughout the services— checking my watch, reading the bulletin, or just looking around the sanctuary. However, I did get interested in a Sunday school class led by Reverend Doug Watson, the Riverside Hospital Chaplain. But, again, this was based on an intellectual, not spiritual, curiosity. I even consented to having Doug perform a private ceremony at Warwick Memorial to renew our marriage vows on our twenty-fifth wedding anniversary. Lastly, I took membership classes and joined the church during one Sunday service; though I still had not made a commitment to Christ.

Even though I was a non-seeker then, seeds were being planted for our move to Williamsburg and my God-seeking mindset at the Williamsburg Community Chapel.

Throughout this time, Cooka and I were unequally yoked, our marriage struggling due to my "heels-dug-in" attitude and her desire to get me into the faith. God intervened in a big way as I, "unexplainably", consented to attend a Marriage Encounter weekend advertised during a Warwick Memorial service. Looking back, I cannot imagine why I said "yes" to this, except for God's direct intervention.

The Marriage Encounter weekend was a wonderful time of learning how to communicate with each other with love based on God's love, and literally "saved" our marriage as it rejuvenated our love for each other. It also, especially at the closing ceremony, included a very touching spiritual message of how God's love connects to marital love. I felt this cloud of the Holy Spirit during that weekend and for a while afterward, before it faded. However, from a marriage standpoint, this was a pivotal event for preserving our relationship in preparation for what was to come . . . faith, ministry and cancer!

In the spring of 1990, when we were considering adding on to our house and I was feeling uncomfortable about putting more cash into a house in Denbigh, we went to Kingsmill in Williamsburg, just to get a feel for the city. During this first visit, we fell in love with a house that was ninety-percent complete and had everything we wanted. After contemplating this purchase, I decided to take the financial risk and bought the house. Taking a risk of this magnitude was very unlike me, and I am now convinced this was God's hand leading me to make this move.

That fall, we moved into our new home and started visiting two Williamsburg churches, Walnut Hills Baptist and Williamsburg Community Chapel. We visited the Chapel more, because I had heard Dick Woodward, senior pastor at that time, speak at a men's breakfast in Newport News in the past. We enjoyed his teaching and I even paid attention to what he was saying most of the time.

I liked associate pastor Bill Warrick, but his preaching then was in a "developmental" stage. Although I was getting the message only from an intellectual standpoint at this stage, it allowed me to relate the Scripture to real life and kept my intellectual interest in God's Word.

One of the VERY important things that happened during the years between Cooka's conversion and mine was that I had observed a positive change in her and how she related to me. Even though she was super-persistent in pushing her faith on the family, I noticed that she was much more loving and respectful of me. We seemed to get along much better, which, in retrospect, was due more to her submissive spirit that anything that I did.

She was living out *1 Peter 3:1-2*

"Wives, likewise, be submissive to your own husbands, that even if some do not obey the word, they, without a word, may be won by the conduct of their wives."

I was being "won" by her love during this important time.

By that spring, God was intervening in several areas of my life in order to lead me toward Him. I had been so interested in Chapel teaching and Dick Woodward's mini-Bible classes that I was becoming more attracted to the Bible. Moreover, I became interested in learning more about this Jesus who had made such a big impact on Cooka's life and our marital relationship.

A little voice in the back of my head said, "Jim, you need to read about Jesus in the Bible if you are going to understand this." One day, I shared my desire to read the Bible with Cooka and a study Bible miraculously appeared on my desk the next day, wrapped like a birthday gift.

Without any suggestions on where to start (surely at this point in my faith journey I wasn't about to call Dick Woodward or Bill Warrick), I began reading the Gospel of Matthew. I was getting facts about Jesus' life, but I did not understand the significance of what I was reading.

Hence, about four weeks later, that same "little voice" told me that I needed to attend the Friday Williamsburg Men's Breakfast if I was going to comprehend what I was reading.

The teaching on Fridays were a great boost to my desire to learn more about Jesus and to start hearing what the Gospel really meant, and how it related to my life. The other important outcome of the Friday breakfasts was that I wanted to spend some one-on-one time with Bill to ask about my many questions and objections to the Gospel.

I was fortunate to have Thursdays off from my practice, and so around June 1993 I started meeting with him and asking some tough questions about my reservations about the Gospel. I had three main objections to accepting the truth about Jesus and the Gospel:

1. The truthfulness of the Resurrection—did Jesus really come back to life after death on the cross?
2. Was eternal life, particularly after becoming a born-again Christian, a reality, or just wishful thinking on the part of Christians?
3. Was Satan real, as an evil creature that roamed the earth and plied us to sin against God, or was this just the natural tendency of man to do evil that led to the bad things of this world?

As a physician, grounded in science, I could not accept resurrection or eternal life. For twenty-three years, I had taken care of terminal lung disease patients and had never witnessed anyone come to life or be resurrected after I pronounced them dead with a flat line EKG. Moreover, my early years in biomedical research led me to look for concrete physical evidence of a profound result such as resurrection, and I never witnessed that in patients.

The skepticism of everlasting life was directly connected to these doubts of resurrected life, which would have to be the first step to living eternally. For my third objection to the Gospel, that of belief in Satan as a real being, since I could not see him or any direct effects in my life, I could find no reason to believe he was authentic.

For many weekly Thursday afternoons, Bill and I discussed these three objections, plus other aspects of the Gospel of which I had no knowledge. During this time, I continued to read the Gospels in my Bible, starting with Matthew. However, not long after starting our meetings, Bill encouraged me to jump over to the Gospel of John, and read that book next.

These studies and discussions of John opened a door of light into my understanding of who Jesus was and what He was saying. To this day, it is my favorite book of the Bible. In addition to my Bible reading, Bill gave me three books to read that were extraordinarily helpful in my quest for faith: *More Than a Carpenter*, by Josh McDowell, *Who Moved the Stone*, by Frank Morrison and C. S. Lewis's *Mere Christianity*.

McDowell's and Morrison's books presented the compelling evidence of Jesus as the Son of God, and, most importantly, convinced me of the truth of His Resurrection.

Since this truth is the central point of the Gospel and the proof of eternal life, I knew that I had to be convinced of its veracity. The conclusive evidence included:

1. Morrison and McDowell's investigative examination of the Gospels showing that the resurrection did occur;
2. The secular Jewish historian Josephus noting in the first century that followers of a certain rabbi from Nazareth claimed he had risen from the dead;
3. If the resurrection story was a conspiracy, then at least one of the twelve apostles would, under the threat of death, have given up that secret. However, all apostles, except John, died as martyrs for not renouncing their faith in Jesus.

Lewis' classic book *Mere Christianity* presented the most persuasive argument for God as a good and loving Father, Jesus as His Son and my Savior, and the undeniable presence of a Dark Power, as Satan, who is constantly engaged in an eternal battle of spiritual warfare against God and His people. Lewis argues convincingly that the Dark Power

> . . . is a mighty evil spirit who was the evil power behind death, disease and sin . . . Christianity thinks this Dark Power was created by God, and was good when he was created, and went wrong. Christianity agrees . . . that the universe is at war.

We are in a civil war, a rebellion, and Satan works day and night as a rebel attacking God's people. Since Satan is a spirit (albeit, a created one—a fallen angel), he is unseen to the human eye, and consequently, non-believers do not believe he exists; a position I held before reading *Mere Christianity*.

But now, I was certain that Satan, as an evil force, was indeed real.

Hence, as a result of reading these books and my Bible, plus my discussions with Bill, I realized in September of that same year that all of my objections to belief had been overcome. At least in my head, I believed that the Gospel was true; Jesus was who He said he was, He was resurrected with the promise of eternal life for believers; and Satan was a real force in the world.

However, I had not made the connection to my heart, and was unwilling at this time to commit my life to Christ. I was "in limbo."

In the spring of that year, my friend Ken Jones reminded me of the November Bermuda retreat that I had agreed to attend with my wife, a year earlier. To this day, this commitment by me remains the greatest evidence for the Providence of God!

I had already turned down two consecutive previous invites to attend a "fun" retreat in Bermuda with the Joneses and several others. The fact that this meeting was about Jesus never crossed my mind as a non-believer.

Bermuda did sound like a neat place for a vacation and Cooka and I had never been there. After three years of declining invitations because the retreat conflicted with hunting or fishing trips, Ken finally was successful in convincing me. Of course, God knew these earlier years would have been counterproductive, because I was seriously entrenched in unbelief. He also knew that my search for faith would not begin until the spring of 1993, and that now I would be "ready" to accept the Good News of Jesus Christ that November in Bermuda.

Carrying my newfound intellectual belief in the truth of the Gospel, we departed for Bermuda on November 10, arriving with more than fifty other couples. My week there was so positively unreal and uplifting, it is hard to express the feelings my heart experienced.

This was, and still remains, the mountaintop experience of my life! The retreat was six days wholly oriented to the living Christ and how His love and our surrender to Him has changed so many people's lives. There was a palpable sensation of Christ's love emanating from everyone at the meeting; this was transforming for me, as I had never had such a feeling at medical or other secular gatherings. I heard the term "Jesus plus nothing" for the first time there. While not understood at first, I came to realize this meant one does not need denominations or creeds, but only a relationship with the risen Savior that is built on God's grace.

On the second night my spiritual awakening occurred when I med Father Joe Grizone. Father Joe was a retired evangelical Catholic priest who presented Jesus as God-man, in the water-to-wine miracle of the Cana wedding. For the first time, I realized from Joe's presentation that Jesus was a real person, loving everything and every person. To me, He was touchable, finite flesh as a man. The miracle of turning water into wine proved His claim to be the Son of God. Hence, I now knew that His death on the cross, and resurrection, was to take my sins on Him, and to return to Heaven at the right hand of God the Father. I was faced with the reality that I could no longer view Jesus and His Gospel as some far off spiritual concept. I *had* to make a choice!

For the rest of that wonderful week, a spiritual battle was raging inside me. The evil forces of Satan were trying to convince me that if I committed my heart to Christ, I could not live up to God's standards of conduct so the life of faith would be a major disappointment. The Spirit of God was convincing me that I had to choose Christ because all the love and personhood of Jesus I was experiencing was indeed real and I knew I wanted that. Because of the Evil voices, I kept procrastinating on a commitment up to and through the last full day. I can remember riding the scooters through Bermuda streets with other friends but being almost paralyzed mentally by the yin-yang of forces working on me.

Not until midnight on November 16 in our bedroom at the Castle Harbor Hotel, did I brush aside the Evil voices. Cooka had no idea what was bothering me, since I did not share the spiritual war in which I was embroiled. She was awestruck when I asked her to kneel with me at the bedside while I prayed the prayer of salvation; asking Christ to forgive my sins, come into my heart and take over my life! Tears of joy fell from both of us, framing this most wonderful moment in our marriage- both finally equally yoked together in Christ.

It was a crisp, sunny fall day when we landed in Norfolk on our return. Still on my mountaintop, I had brought tears to Kendal Jones' eyes when I told him and his wife Nancy of my commitment the night before. We had a wonderful reception from Travis and Ashley, both of whom were at home when we walked through the front door. Because they were non-believers, I did not share much with them about my surrender to Christ on return, and regret it to this day. But I remained on a joyous high, and the kids could tell something was different in me, though they never asked me why.

Not many days later, the devil attacked. There were arguments with Travis and Ashley, as well as extra stresses at work. In spite of this, I was undeterred in my pursuit of more information and more relationship with Him. I never missed a Friday men's breakfast, and in my Thursday meetings with Bill Warrick, I suddenly understood more of his explanation of the Gospel than ever before. The Holy Spirit had given me, at salvation, ears to hear and a heart to understand His Word. In my men's small group I was more intentional in my attendance and study.

Probably most important of all was that Cooka and I were now fully on the same page spiritually! This enhanced our marriage relationship to a level never before present. We both attained a zenith of love for each other that was manifested as God's type of love. This was made possible by the agape love we individually felt from our relationship with Jesus. I am convinced that our mutual surrender to Jesus saved our troubled marriage and was the primary factor in our love relationship still growing today.

On the Thursday following our return from Bermuda, I met with Bill for our usual time. I wanted to keep him in some suspense about what happened, so I told him how great the golf, the scooter riding, the weather, the new friends were. Then finally I said, "And, I got on my knees with Cooka the last night and committed my life to Christ."

He came over with tears in his eyes and gave me a big hug . . . and that was when I realized that Bill had hung in there with me at those meetings, Thursday after Thursday, as he was "fishing" for me, befriending me, waiting for the Spirit to move me over the line; which it did at midnight on November 16, 1993.

Being "on fire for the Lord," I wanted to proclaim my faith publicly. Cooka and I decided to wait for our baptism until Easter 1994. We met with the Elders in Dick Woodward's home in March 1994 and gave our testimonies to obtain membership in the Williamsburg Community Chapel.

Approximately two weeks later on April 3, we were baptized together in the Chapel baptismal pool by our good friend and Pastor Tuck Knupp. What a wonderful moment for both of us! I can still remember the awesome feeling of sitting on the back row of the Chapel; wet hair, dressed, but still slightly damp. Watching the remaining baptisms, knowing that all of our friends and even the congregants, who did not know us, had heard us proclaim our faith and surrender to Christ.

THE LEFT RAIL: PROVIDENCE

"Each one should use whatever gift he has received to serve others, faithfully administering God's grace in its various forms." ~1 Pet. 4:10

Now, let's focus on the left-side rail of the railway track: the Lackey Free Clinic ministry.

I remember Dick Woodward saying many times that the Providence of God was like a Hebrew newspaper—that you had to read it backwards in order to understand it. Only by looking backwards can I even have a hint of understanding His Providence in my life, both before and after salvation.

God knew that I would need all of the medical training I obtained by moving around the U.S. and that I would come to faith that night in November 1993. Although, "who can know the mind of God?" I suspect that He had in His mind that I, with my "on fire" desire to give back to Christ, would try to start a free clinic in Lackey with my wife.

Believing the Biblical teaching that God is omniscient, I am certain that He knew that I would develop multiple myeloma cancer in my cervical spine some four years later. As a matter of fact, He knew that the pains I experienced in my neck on the tennis court during our second Bermuda retreat were that of the cancer in its early stage. Our all-knowing Father knew that without Christ or Cooka at my side, I would not have been able to weather the horrendous storm of cancer, the radiation, and radical neck surgery, and tolerate the halo for three months.

He also knew that the cancer would be a means to take me out of my busy pulmonary practice and give me the extended times of remission necessary to be His hands and feet in shepherding the Lackey Free Clinic ministry to further His Kingdom. Through these years of cancer battle and ministry growth, He has taught me the *extreme* value of patience and perseverance; to never, ever give up, as long as I know that I am doing His Will and being led by His Holy Spirit.

The Spirit carried us through much spiritual warfare, including relapses and the necessity of stem cell transplant in 2003; the blessing of our Mayo Clinic doctor, Dr. Martha Lacy; the years of few or no patients attending the original Thursday night Lackey clinics; the barriers that Satan put up through county bureaucrats delaying our original building construction, and each subsequent Lackey Free Clinic expansion; and the troubled exit of three executive directors and two medical directors (but God had better plans with each change).

In all of this, God has expanded the ministry to make Lackey a place of Christ's joy and love for our staff, volunteers, and patients. It has become an oasis of His hope for the many hopeless patients we encounter. Along with this, Lackey has been recognized in Virginia's free clinic world as one of the best-organized clinics, and has won nearly every volunteer award offered by local government, media and foundation organizations; in some cases more than once.

I didn't know any of this back in 1993, following the Bermuda retreat but my Heavenly Father did! Starting the first day after returning home, I had a burning desire to somehow give back to God what Jesus had done for me by granting me forgiveness and salvation through His death on the cross.

This time, as I devoured the New Testament and the Gospels, I read the verse from Matthew which says, **"In as much as you do it unto the least of these my brethren, you do it unto me"** (Matthew 25:40).

When I read this verse, a light bulb went on and I knew I had to give back to Him for what he did for me. I had good medical skills that I had acquired through the years of training and practice. Why not use these skills to serve the poor? This revelation birthed the idea to somehow start offering free medical care to those who needed but could not afford it.

**Being a good doctor, I figured that I could serve
Jesus by offering my medical services to "the least
of these," the disadvantaged and the indigent
that were in the Lackey community.**

At this time a concept of a clinic or a large organization like the Lackey Free Clinic was nowhere in our thinking. I started looking for a location to serve. Unfortunately, it took some time for me to find the God-intended location. There were many doors that seemed to be closed during the search. First, I tried to inquire with churches in downtown Newport News, since that area had a high poverty level on the Peninsula. However, not a single church ever called me back. Next, I had an interview with Old Town Medical Clinic in Williamsburg. At that interview, I learned that the Clinic did not have any Thursday afternoon or evening times available for me to volunteer; and at that time they were only seeing gynecological/obstetrical patients, an area in which I obviously had no expertise.

During my search, word reached Walter Johnson, the pastor of Zion Prospect Baptist Church off of Route 17 in York County. Pastor Johnson met me in the Riverside Hospital cafeteria to discuss ideas for where I might locate a free clinic. Walter was aware of a low income area of York County called Lackey which, as far as he knew, had very limited access to medical care. As it turned out, Lackey was the lowest socio-economic area in the York County, James City, and Williamsburg area.

I asked, "Where's Lackey?" Once Pastor Johnson had explained the geography and some of the socio-economic aspects of the area, I made calls to three different churches. The only one to return the call was Pastor James Tabb, Sr. from Rising Sun Baptist Church, a 100-plus-year-old church with an African-American congregation.

Sometime in December 1994, I met with Pastor Tabb and the deacons of the church after a Wednesday night Bible study, explaining that I wanted to come serve the poor and use their facility on Thursday evenings. Pastor Tabb was positive about this, but a couple of the deacons were suspicious that there was an ulterior motive for a white physician to come into a black community out of the blue, making an offer to serve, without any prompting. I explained to them that I had no other reason beyond purely wanting to serve Christ.

It was decided that the initial meeting would occur the first Thursday following Easter. The church agreed to let us use a large open Sunday school room in the rear of the church behind the sanctuary. We asked Pastor Tabb and the deacons if they would put out an announcement about the clinic opening and the need for help—any nurses or related workers who might be in the congregation.

Within a week or two, we heard from Mrs. Russell Lockley.

Mrs. Lockley was a wonderful 70ish-year-old African American lady who had one of the most positive attitudes that we have ever been around. She was a real cheerleader for us throughout the early days of the clinic and she knew everybody in the church and most of the people in the community. This made her the perfect liaison for us within Lackey—another one of God's provisions.

The first meeting of the clinic occurred on the evening of April 20, 1995. We met in the large Bible study/Sunday school room in the back of the church, which had an adjacent kitchen where meals were served when the congregation got together on Sundays after church. It also had a small, approximately six-by-nine-foot room that was called the library, though it had very few books, and it was used primarily by the deacons and the treasurer for counting the Sunday collections. This library room became an examination room in order to provide the patients some privacy.

Rising Sun Baptist Church, Lackey, Virginia

Initially the room had only a chair in which we could examine the patients, but eventually we were able to get Riverside Hospital to donate a used examination table.

As Cooka and I were planning the start up at Rising Sun, we envisioned that we would be overrun with people coming in for medical care. We planned to open the clinic between six and nine in the evening, but anticipated that because of the large number of patients, we might have to stay past 10 p.m.

As we would soon learn, this was a gross overestimation. Not a single patient showed that first night!

On the door was a poster board sign that said, "Free Clinic 6 to 9 p.m." written in magic marker. Week after week, we sat there with only an occasional patient. Many nights, the only people we would see were those of the church choir entering through the rear door on their way to practice in the sanctuary. Every now and then, one, two or three would stop to have their blood pressure checked, or to have me check a skin rash. (If only they knew how poor a dermatologist this pulmonary doc was.)

This continued for the next year and a half. Many nights were spent discussing the weather and things going on in Mrs.

Lockley's life. Cooka often used this time to write notes, do needlepoint, or some Bible reading.

This was a challenging time of great disappointment for us. However, Mrs. Lockley was our constant cheerleader as she would always say, "Now don't you go getting all discouraged. When God is ready, He'll bring the people here. Don't get discouraged. You got to wait on the Lord."

Cooka and I would often discuss why we were not getting patients. At one point, we moved the sign out to the marquee for the church; again it was a pitiful cardboard poster sign. This sign would sometimes be put up a day before the clinic, so that people riding down the main Route 238 would see it. We also contacted York County and they put a notice up about the free medical care at Rising Sun in a seniors' newsletter that was distributed throughout the area. Additionally, we put notices on the bulletin boards at the local laundry mats and in two federally-subsidized housing projects in the area.

Still, no patients came.

At this time I was studying Henry Blackaby's book *Experiencing God.* As emphasized by Dr. Blackaby, sometimes we run ahead of God's plan for our life. Was God's plan for us to hold the free clinic somewhere else or had He something else in mind for us to serve Him? We decided on two different occasions during those subsequent two and a half years that we were going to test God by offering a Gideon's fleece (Judges Chapters 6-8) challenge to Him. We set two closing dates for the clinic, and prayed that God would let us know what HIS will would be for us regarding the clinic's continuation. If He did not want us to continue, we would experience the same low patient load; or, if He wanted us to continue, He would provide patients for us to indicate that we were to stay at Rising Sun.

In each instance, almost miraculously within two to three weeks of the closing date, God brought many patients in the door. However, after a few weeks of heavy patient attendance, in both instances it slowed to a trickle once again.

In the late summer, we were approached by York County regarding moving the clinic to a community center which was under construction in Charles Brown Park, approximately a quarter-mile west of the church. We were very excited about this proposal. The facility was a much better design for providing care, with one of the rooms being more like a medical office with a sink and locked cabinet. I would no longer have to carry my supplies back and forth in a cardboard box.

In October of that same year, we moved to the Charles Brown Community Center. We were so excited about the new facility and hopeful that patients would soon be coming there regularly. At the same time though, we were a bit sad to leave the church, since we had developed a good rapport with the choir members practicing on Thursday nights. We would definitely miss the praise music!

The Community Center was a wonderful facility. The rent was zero and it was a great place to have the clinic operating with all volunteer workers and donated resources, including medical supplies and physicians' samples. There was a large multipurpose room which we set up with chairs, a registration table, and folding screens behind which patients were screened by the nursing volunteers. As the clinic grew over the years at Charles Brown, we developed a rolling chart storage system and acquired a mobile computer and printer, as well as other equipment; all stored in the main exam room, packed like sardines in a can and rolled out by volunteer staff prior to starting registration for the clinic.

Charles Brown Park Community Center

We were a true MASH unit with a wonderful cadre of volunteers who enthusiastically set up our clinic each Thursday night, and later on Monday mornings when we opened our second clinic session.

It was shortly thereafter, in 1997, when tragedy struck on that July day when the MRI at Riverside Hospital showed bone cancer in my spine. Within a few days of this, we had signs put up on the Community Center door saying that the clinic was closed. Cooka and I assumed that the clinic dream was finished because of the severity of the cancer and the complexity of the planned treatment, with the results of that treatment unknown.

As discussed earlier, I underwent radiation therapy followed by emergency surgery at the University of Virginia to remove the cancer in my spine and fuse the vertebrae together.

On January 13 1998, I returned to my pulmonary practice at Riverside, and began seeing my first patients since my diagnosis seven months earlier. By early February, I was feeling fairly comfortable in a cervical collar and felt a strong calling to return to Charles Brown Community Center to reopen the clinic. In retrospect, it seems crazy that I would do this while my neck was still immobilized. It honestly made no sense, but obviously God, through the Holy Spirit, was leaning on me heavily at that time.

Upon returning the first evening to reopen the clinic, we were dismayed that the former examination room and equipment cabinet had been broken into and several pieces of our original equipment were missing. My first reaction on seeing the door hanging halfway off the equipment cabinet was that of sorrow and disbelief. Why would someone break in and steal medical equipment that they could not use and rob the community of certain free medical services provided by this equipment?

But, I knew that God, through His Spirit, had directed us back to this ministry. I also knew that Satan did not want us delivering the love of Jesus through free medical care in this building. Therefore, we were undaunted and even more resolved to re-equip the room and open the doors to the hurting poor. The Clinic reopened in mid-February 1998.

We again faced the problem of few, if any, patients. However, we were committed to serve God here in Lackey, and redoubled our efforts to get the word out through York County and the local housing projects. Eventually patients came, and through my practice in Riverside Hospital, I challenged nurses and doctors to come out and volunteer. Gradually, a group of nurses and a few physicians came regularly to volunteer.

Among the first volunteer physicians were Dr. Claire McCracken, family practice; Dr. Stan Yeatts, gynecology; Dr. Richard Brzeski, pediatrics; and also Dr. George Griggs, pulmonary/internal medicine.

With clinical activity picking up at the Charles Brown Community Center, we felt it was time to become more structured as an organization. We had already received the IRS 501(c)3 designation in 1998, which allowed us to operate as a nonprofit organization, but we had never really had a true board of directors.

On January 10, 2000, the first board members met and were elected; the members included Dr. Christina Swenson; Dan Johnson, nurse-anesthetist; Dr. George Griggs; Mr. David Otey, attorney; James Wharton, pharmacist; Mary and William Giles and Charles Fitzgerald from Rising Sun Church; and Walter Johnson, Pastor of Zion Prospect Baptist Church. At that time officers were elected and included President Jim Shaw, Vice President Dan Johnson, Treasurer Dr. Christina Swenson, and Secretary Cooka Shaw.

At this time, we also recognized the overcrowding situation and the ever-present lack of privacy for patients and physicians at the community center. Consequently, we saw the need to seek funding to rent another building or build our own facility.

Since 1998, we had been operating the Clinic on approximately $1,200 savings, which had been given by the Williamsburg Community Chapel and a friend. This paltry sum had been used to obtain supplies and pharmaceutical samples to meet patient's' needs. However, we realized that a busy clinic needed more funding.

Accordingly, in December 1999, prior to the first board meeting, we sent out an appeal letter to several hundred friends and volunteers of the Clinic. That appeal letter, by God's grace, collected more than $25,000, resulting in a bank balance of $26,608 by the first board meeting in January 2000.

Another Providential miracle occurred at the June board meeting later that year. This meeting was held at Rising Sun Church instead of the community center. Mr. William Washington, a community leader and a Rising Sun deacon, was invited to attend. During the discussion about the possibility of a new building for Lackey Clinic, he noted that he had available for purchase a piece of land that was approximately a quarter of a mile from the church right on Route 238, or Old Williamsburg Road.

At that same meeting, Mrs. Mary Giles, member of Rising Sun Church and the Board of Directors, agreed to petition the York County Volunteer Association for potential donations to help finance the purchase of the land. I, along with Cooka and the board, knew that it was a big stretch to consider buying a piece of land when we would also need to raise the money to finance the construction of a medical building. However, as shown in the clinic history up to this point, God had His own plan for expanding the Clinic to bring Christ's love to those in need on the Virginia Peninsula.

The year 2000 was a pivotal and active year for the Lackey Free Clinic. In August, a grant submission to Riverside Health Foundation and also to the Bernadine Franciscan Sisters Foundation was approved. With this, we were able to hire Marianne McKee as our first Executive Director. Marianne had a heart for serving the poor in Jesus' name, and was extremely energetic in helping the Clinic get organized in moving towards the possibility of our own facility.

As we saw the Clinic grow, we realized that we could not meet all the patient needs on Thursday evenings alone. We reached a point where we were seeing twenty-five to thirty patients on some nights, and I was beginning to burn out some of my volunteer physicians with such large patient loads. Dr. Christina Swenson stepped forward and took the initiative to set up a Monday morning clinic, where she and a scattered number of retired physicians volunteered to see patients. The Monday Clinic opened on September 11, 2000, and added tremendously to the number of patients we were able to reach by offering expert medical care and the love of Christ.

From the outset, the *modus operandi* of the Clinic was to provide excellent, top-notch care that was at least as good as most of the primary care practices in the area, as well as to show the love of Christ by treating our patients with compassion, love and restoration of dignity. As the "left brain" part of the Founder team, I sought to bring excellence to the diagnosis and treatment of patients' problems and to provide this in a compassionate, tender, and non-hurried environment. Cooka, with her upbeat, outgoing Christ-centered personality, engaged each patient right from the start in the waiting room with loving, caring conversation, allaying their fear and anxiety. These anxieties were most often caused by dysfunctional home situations that bred financial and relational hardships.

Due to their lack of health insurance, these patients were usually turned away from physicians' offices.

Love and Compassion for patients

The Lord is gracious and full of compassion, Slow to anger and great in mercy, The Lord is good to all, and His tender mercies are over all His works. ~ Ps. 145: 8-9

Mrs. B. was a Chinese-American woman, married to an abusive former soldier. She came to the clinic in tears. She noted symptoms of depression, including insomnia, chronic exhaustion, and sadness. Her history was taken by a caring clinic nurse, who listened attentively and compassionately to not only her medical complaints, but also her pain from having no support system since her family was in China, her low self-esteem, and no local friends.

She was seen by a volunteer physician, her gynecological and physical complaints were addressed, and follow-up appointments were made. When she was ready for discharge, she was given reassuring hugs by the nursing staff. She smiled and said, "I have never experienced such a wonderful reception in a doctor's office. Thank you so much." She was followed up for two years, experiencing marked improvement in her depression on medication. The Clinic went the extra mile and connected her with a Chinese couple in her neighborhood to meet which developed into a supportive relationship.

Mrs. B's experience is what we endeavored to do from the early beginnings of the Clinic : to show the patient the love for the "least of these" that was commanded by Jesus. We do not force the Gospel on any of our patients but we make sure that we communicate through Scriptures on the walls, comments on why we are here (to serve Christ), and offerings of optional prayer, they know we are serving them because of our love for Jesus Christ. We follow the principle attributed to St. Francis of Assisi, "Preach the Gospel, and if necessary, use words." We want our actions to be the hands and feet of Jesus to our patients.

And whatever you do in word or deed, do all in the name of the Lord Jesus, giving thanks to God the Father through Him. ~ Col. 3:17

The second most important principle for treating our patients has been to offer top-notch medical and dental care in a manner that, as stated in Colossians above, would honor the Name of Jesus Christ. As a result, we have attracted the best volunteer physicians in our community and obtained superb support from our local hospital systems for access to up-to-date lab and x-ray testing. We strive to obtain a level of care that is similar to the regular offices and clinics in our community.

Wanda was a 23-year-old heroin and cocaine addict who came to the Clinic with complaints of fever and fatigue. She had been in and out of jail both for narcotic possession and assault, and had just been released. Patiently taking her history, I was not deterred by her foul language. Noticing the needle tracks on her arms from heroin injections and deciding she needed a complete exam, I discovered that she had a fever and a soft heart murmur (an abnormal sound caused by a sick heart valve).

She was sent to the hospital lab for cultures of her blood and other blood tests. Four days later the lab called to notify me of bacteria in her blood. This confirmed my suspicion that she had an infection of her heart valve, caused by injections with dirty needles. This condition is called subacute bacterial endocarditis, which can be lethal if not treated.

A phone call to a cardiology friend at the hospital got her additional tests to confirm the diagnosis, and she was admitted for life-saving intravenous antibiotic therapy.

Wanda is a great example of our goal to provide superior diagnostic and treatment services and not cut corners just because we are a free clinic. In some settings, because of her addiction and hardened attitude, she might have been turned away or just given an antibiotic and sent out without an adequate assessment of her illness. Jesus was relentless in his concern for the poor ("the last shall be first and the first shall be last." Mark 10:31), and He challenges us to offer the very best to those like Wanda, who are at the bottom of the barrel.

Therefore go and make disciples of all nations,
baptizing them in the name of the Father and of the
Son and of the Holy Spirit . . . ~Matt. 28:19

Ultimately, our purpose at the Clinic is to spread the Gospel of Jesus Christ. We have felt that God has called us to use a "soft" method. This includes, most importantly, showing the love of Jesus, making Him and His Gospel attractive to these brokenhearted patients. But it also comprises other components.

"I'm going to court next week and probably will be going to jail again," revealed Wanda, visibly distraught, on her second clinic visit. After listening to more details, I said, "You know, Wanda, when I really get in a tough situation, I look in the Bible for comfort and peace. Why don't you take one of our free Bibles with you and read in Psalms and the book of John?"

Three months later, Wanda returned for a follow up. She was excited to tell me that she had taken the Bible to jail, studied it, and asked Jesus to come into her life. Not only that, but she said that she led a Bible study with other female inmates at the jail! Imagine the joy for Cooka and I and the other volunteers that had served Wanda. We were ecstatic that God had used us to help bring Wanda into the Kingdom.

We feel it is a key part of our mission to have available copies of God's Word for those patients who wanted them. Thanks to a generous donor, we have given away several hundred Bibles over the past fourteen years.

"I knew I was in a place of compassion and peace when I walked in the door and saw the Bible verses on the walls," wrote Sue in her thank you letter to the Clinic. Having the Word written on the walls and available for patients to take has been a great follow up when patients question why we are serving-- to obey Jesus' command in the Bible.

A Constant Stream of Blessings

*"Blessed is the one who has regard for the weak; the
Lord delivers him in time of trouble."* ~ Ps. 41:1

With a steady increase in patient visits and a growing team
of nurse and physician volunteers, things began to move along
over the ensuing six months toward obtaining a new clinic
building. On April 3, 2001, after having been petitioned by
Mary Giles and me, the York County Volunteer Association
agreed to donate $30,000 to purchase the land for the new
clinic building.

What a miracle from God!

The board of directors and volunteer staff were overwhelmed
by the grace from God that enabled this first giant step toward
the possibility of a new facility for the clinic.

In the fall of that year, after much hard work by Colleen
Robertson, Marianne McKee, and a large volunteer staff, our
first dinner and auction fundraiser was held at the Newport
News Ramada Inn. Mr. Bobby Beck, a longtime friend of mine,
kindly provided the facility and the meal as a donation to the
clinic. We raised $48,000 that night—*another miracle*!

Based upon the wonderful results from the fundraiser, plus
the other commitments that the board and I had obtained from
the community and various foundations in the area, we could
look at our financial situation to see if we now had the funds to
proceed with the building plans.

In late December, a key meeting was held at Ukrops Café
in Williamsburg with board members Gary Fernandez, Chuck
Ream and I. I called this meeting because Board sentiment
was that we did not have enough funds to pay for the building.
Following God's repeated call in Scripture to persevere when

following his commands, I was not going to be deterred by a negative outlook from the Board.

After reviewing the current funds available, both in hand and committed, I was able to convince them that there would be enough to finance the entire project. The funding for the project was then recommended and approved at the next full board meeting.

Later that month, Leon Smith, an architect from Newport News, submitted revised building plans for the new building. Shortly thereafter, Donald Davis and Associates, civil engineers, started working on the site plan *pro bono* for the Lackey clinic ministry. At the same time, Dan and Fred Nice from Nice Construction Company started getting bids from subcontractors for the project.

Clinic visits continued to increase at the Charles Brown Community Center, while funds were obtained for the building construction at 1620 Old Williamsburg Road. The land was formally purchased from the estate of William Washington with the $30,000 grant provided by York County Volunteer Association.

Finally on July 18, 2002, with great celebration, we held the groundbreaking ceremony for the new Lackey Free Clinic building. The ceremony was attended by all York County Supervisors, the board members and donors, and clinic volunteers.

We were overwhelmed with God's providential blessing. It was hard for us to believe that only six years earlier, we were sitting alone in the back of Rising Sun Baptist Church with no one coming in the door for medical attention. Now, here we were breaking ground for a new clinic facility with paid staff and a large cadre of volunteers!

August 9, 2003
We moved into our brand new
3,150 sq. ft. clinic building debt free!!!

Once negotiations with York County over setbacks and zoning issues with the new site plan were completed, construction began in the fall of 2002. On August 9, 2003, a dedication and grand opening was held for the new 3,150-square-foot clinic building. This was most definitely an incredibly joyful moment for everyone involved in the clinic. The ceremony was held in the parking lot adjacent to the clinic, and the keynote message was delivered by Pastor Bill Warwick. Praise the Lord! God is so good!

Within one week of opening the new clinic facility, we hired the first part-time, salaried nurse practitioner. This allowed us to have coverage for two Walk-in Clinics, on Monday morning and Thursday evening, and also for one all day Chronic Care Clinic. The chronic care clinics were dedicated to patients with at least one chronic medical condition and were held by appointment only. As a result, the Clinic was now providing services three days a week as opposed to one half-day and one evening per week as before.

The joy that we felt at the grand opening celebration was tempered by knowing my multiple myeloma cancer was getting worse. I had been on chemotherapy since April 2003 and knew that I would soon need an autologous stem cell transplant. On September 22, 2003, I entered the Medical College of Virginia's

Bone Marrow Transplant Center and underwent chemotherapy followed by a stem cell transplant using my own stem cells.

This was a difficult, rigorous, and painful form of therapy which necessitated a two-week hospitalization and then six more weeks of residency in the Richmond area for follow up by the Bone Marrow Transplant Clinic. Because of the risks of acquiring infections from the community, I was instructed not to participate in group activities and was kept out of Clinic and board activities until February 2004.

The clinic continued to operate at a high quality level thanks to the leadership of Marianne McKee and the Board, chaired by Vice President Kendall Jones. By God's grace, I was able to return to board leadership in February and also to start filling the role of medical director in short visits. This gradually increased over the next two to three months until I was able to assume full-time medical director duties.

Over the next few years, the Clinic continued to expand as God brought resources and volunteers, as well as salaried staff, to the ministry of carrying His love to the aching patients who appeared at Lackey's doors.

This growth included Kay Bradley, succeeding Marianne McKee as executive director in August. This same year, the dental clinic opened with Josh Lachine, DDS, as dental director. In another blessing from God, the funds for the purchase of the equipment for one dental operatory were provided by unsolicited donations from the Yorktown Business Persons Association. We will forever be grateful to Mr. Junior Coxton, a local businessman, who was instrumental in obtaining the funds for the dental operatory.

God continued to provide funds for operating expenses at the Clinic. The dinner and auction in October 2004 raised an amazing $103,000. Since the Clinic was getting very busy, a budget of $260,000 was approved for 2005! This was hard for us to grasp—that God had grown and blessed His ministry so much.

As the Clinic took care of more and more sick patients with chronic conditions, it became apparent that we needed better access to laboratory, x-ray, and pharmacy services. In April 2005, through the generosity of Riverside Regional Health System, we were provided a charity care agreement that included all laboratory, imaging, and pharmaceuticals at no cost to Clinic patients. This was of **incredible value**, not only in monetary terms, but also in enabling the Clinic to provide more complete, up-to-date care for these patients who otherwise would not receive any care at all.

In May 2005, the Chronic Care Clinics were expanded to an additional full day, allowing us to provide three Chronic Care Clinics per week, plus two Walk-In Clinics.

We had long envisioned an onsite Lackey Clinic chaplain during clinic hours. We hoped that the chaplain would provide spiritual and emotional counseling, and, when appropriate, introduce these hurting patients to the Gospel.

The first chaplain, John Yost, started volunteering on August 19, 1999, while we were in Charles Brown Community Center. John was an interesting and wonderful man who had been a pastor and also a former Philadelphia street cop. He was able to relate to patients at all levels because of his dual past careers. Following John's service, Mel Rosche, retired NASA engineer and founder of the Williamsburg Young Life chapter, became the Clinic Chaplain. Both John and Mel made it part of their chaplain activities to roam about the waiting room at Charles Brown, talking and praying with patients who had spiritual and counseling needs.

However, when we moved to the new Clinic building, we lacked a chaplain volunteer. During this time, we were praying for the funds to have a salaried chaplain available during most of the clinic times. Up until October 2005, there was no funding available for hiring a chaplain, however, that month God blessed the Clinic again.

Cooka and I entertained visitors from England and Ireland who were in the United States to attend the National Prayer Breakfast in Washington, D.C. Two of our guests requested a tour of the Clinic, and at the last minute an Irish member of the Prayer Breakfast group decided to come along. After touring the Clinic, everyone was overwhelmingly impressed with the Clinic and its mission to carry Christ's love to the poor.

As we left the Clinic, while walking to the car, the "last minute" Irish guest revealed that he was an executive director of the Christ-centered Thompson Foundation in Belfast. He asked what our most pressing need was and I replied that it was for a chaplain. He said that he would take our need back to his board when he returned to Ireland.

Not thinking that anything would ever come of this, we found ourselves overwhelmed when one month later we received a letter and a check for the equivalent of $5,000 from the Thompson Foundation, for the chaplain position.

Don Swope, a Christian Missionary Alliance church planter, had shown interest in being a chaplain at the Clinic after I told him of our need. When the seed money was provided by the Thompson Foundation, the Clinic was able to get commitments from several local churches for the remaining funds, and Chaplain Don Swope was hired.

What a wonderful blessing this was for the Clinic and especially for the patients! Chaplain Don spent his time roaming the waiting room, counseling patients and praying with them in his small office adjacent to the waiting room. At times, he was able to present the Gospel to patients and many of them accepted Jesus as their Lord and Savior. Chaplain Swope became an integral part of the vision to deliver expert, compassionate health care in a way that demonstrated the love of Christ.

Fast forward three years, because we were already crowded in our 3,100 square foot building, we were able to add a 1,000 square foot administrative section onto the back of the building. That year we also started an endowment and capital campaign with the help of the Curtis Group in Virginia Beach. This campaign started in the silent phase in 2006 and 2007 but by 2010 was ultimately able to raise $1.2 million.

That same year, the Lackey team provided important leadership in developing a collaborative, non-profit organization called Project Care. It included Peninsula free clinics, local physicians, and three hospital systems—Sentara, Riverside, and Bon Secours. Project Care was designed to recruit specialty physicians to volunteer their services *pro bono* for our clinic patients in their offices.

The hospital systems themselves provided free lab, imaging, physical therapy, and other patient services. Several Lackey Clinic workers were part of the Project Care founding team. This collaborative still provides specialist medical and surgical consultation, and referrals for hospital imaging and lab services.

In May 2007, the Williamsburg Community Foundation, a longtime supporter of the Lackey Free Clinic, formed the Chronic Care Collaborative. This was a collaborative group of free clinics and other health care providers who receive Community Foundation grants. It was coordinated by Health Care Solutions of Richmond with a mission of collaborating and sharing resources in order to improve the health of the medically disadvantaged on the upper and middle peninsulas. The group meets monthly and has been able to share resources and improve the organization and delivery of care through all the participants in the collaborative. This group is a model for cooperation between safety net providers in regions with definite need for indigent health care.

By November, it was obvious that there was once again need to expand our current 4,100-square-foot facility to meet the need of the ever-increasing number of patients seeking our services. In accord with this, the property owner next to the clinic offered to sell his house and the adjacent property. This was accomplished within the same month.

By January 2008, services and the cost of operating the clinic had expanded dramatically, to the point that our annual budget was now $1,036,000. Over *six million* dollars of free health services were provided to the Peninsula community; $6 of free health services were provided for every $1 of Clinic operating funds spent. Praise the Lord!

Because of my persistent issues with cancer and multiple myeloma, in late 2006 God gave the vision to the board to form a task force to explore a transition from a founder-led organization to a board-led organization. Finally, in August 2008, I resigned as a board president and was replaced by one of our faithful RNs.

At the same time, we were also in the process of transitioning me out of the medical director position and raising the funds necessary to hire a salaried medical director that I could train and integrate into the leadership of the clinical services.

Following a lengthy search process, Cattrell Owens, MD, was hired as the first salaried medical director in July 2009. Dr. Owens served for a year, then the role was filled by several part-time directors. Finally in June 2012, Ralph Robertson, MD, was hired as the full-time medical director. He had stepped down as director of the emergency room of Mary Immaculate Hospital. We believe God directed Dr. Robertson to this position, as he had been a faithful volunteer physician at the clinic for over twelve years. He himself felt that he had been nudged by the Holy Spirit to step down from his Emergency Room position in order lead Lackey Clinic medical services as medical director.

In line with our goal of excellence, in November 2008, Lackey Free Clinic was one of the first three clinics in the state of Virginia to be accredited by the Virginia Association of Free Clinics. Moreover, the Clinic received several awards from various foundations, including the Governor's office.

The Lackey Free Clinic won the Governor's Volunteerism and Community Services Award twice, the Virginia Healthcare Foundation's Unsung Healthcare Hero Award three times, as well as awards given by the Williamsburg Community Health Foundation and other local health foundations. There remains a constant focus on being excellent in what we do, both as individuals and as care providers for the hurting poor that come to us.

In May 2011, as a result of negotiations with Riverside Health System, electronic medical records were implemented and first used with our patients in a Chronic Care Clinic. Riverside Health System provided the extensive staff training required for many months prior to that implementation. We finally discontinued paper chart and moved to all-electronic records in October 2013. The Clinic was then one of only a few clinics in the state to use electronic medical records exclusively for the care of its patients.

Dr. Robertson initiated a scribe program to aid physicians who had no experience with electronic health records, particularly those within the system used by Riverside. A scribe coordinator was hired by the Clinic in June 2012, and now the program boasts over fifteen volunteer scribes with one paid coordinator. Each scribe is paired with a physician or nurse practitioner. The scribe, who enters the exam room with the physician or nurse practitioner, records all of the history and physical, diagnostic assessment and plan of care in the electronic medical record under the supervision of the provider. The record is checked and edited on the computer by the physician and is then signed off as the final medical record for that visit.

As with previous growth spurts experienced at the Clinic, it became evident in 2008 that we needed to consider another expansion. As a result, the Holy Spirit prompted the board to consult with a site engineer for possibilities of a building expansion onto the adjacent property purchased in 2007. Concurrently, Guernsey Tingle Architects of Williamsburg was consulted and hired to design a new 6,000-square-foot addition to the current facility. To assist this new capital expansion, funds from the original endowment and capital campaign were to be set aside for the expansion. However, this revealed the need to raise additional funds to provide operating expenses for both the current size of the Clinic as well as for operations when the Clinic expanded. Consequently, the Benevon fundraising model was adopted by the Clinic in February 2009. This model involved providing tours to potential donors at least twice monthly followed by a fundraising luncheon. Our first three Clinic luncheons successfully received between $190,000 and $300,000 in gifts and pledges.

Praise the Lord again!

After a two-year negotiation with York County planners and the Virginia Department of Transportation, groundbreaking for the new building addition took place in May 2012. It was a wonderful event demonstrating the providence of God and the patience the Holy Spirit gave the board during this lengthy time of negotiations.

Final plans for the building included not only the 6,000-square-foot addition, but a total remodel of the original

4,000-square-foot facility that had been used for the previous five years. The new addition was named after Floyd D. Gottwald (Cooka's uncle) whose family had made major financial contributions supporting the construction of the new addition.

By July 2012, the foundation for the new addition was completed and framing had begun.

From my journal, September 11, 2012:

"So many great things happening—the building addition is going great guns with structure, roof and windows in. So exciting for me—Lord, I pray you go before me to try to raise donations we need to complete the project."

In April 2013, this part of the construction phase was complete. The administrative staff and volunteers moved into the new space to allow for remodeling of the old, original space, which would provide new medical and dental examination facilities.

This was a challenging time for our staff and volunteers, as we tried to keep our clinical services running while construction was going on all around us. It limited the number of patients we could see, but thankfully, the incredible perseverance and upbeat attitude of our medical personnel and helpful administrative staff kept services running continually during this phase of construction.

Imagine stepping over a two-by-four wall stud to get into your exam room to see a patient; or trying to listen to heart sounds through your stethoscope with a Skill saw buzzing six feet away.

In spite of noise and various construction-related obstructions, we only had to shut down for two weeks prior to the final move into the newly completed medical and dental part of the facility.

As a result of this wonderful effort, the new Clinic's grand opening in October 2013 celebrated ten medical examination rooms and five dental operatory rooms. The dental clinic had all new up-to-date equipment including electronic medical records and digital x-rays.

The medical clinic was blessed with its own cardiac lab, including an echo machine (measures blood flow and heart muscle efficiency) gifted by Sentara Williamsburg Medical Center and the blessing of a volunteer cardiologist and his wife who were both specialists in echocardiography. We also got a special camera to take pictures of the back of the eye, or retina, in order to greatly increase the number of diabetics screened for disease of the retina.

This new facility was yet another miracle from God. We praise Him and pray that we remain in His will, providing care in a manner that honors the name of Jesus.

The Latest Expansion

THE RIGHT RAIL:
GREATEST BATTLE
OF MY LIFE

"... the battle is the Lord's ..." ~ *1 Sam. 17:47b*

Once the devastating MRI findings were communicated to my neurosurgeon, Dr. Griffith, a chest x-ray was ordered to be sure this was not lung cancer spreading to my spine. I was then sent to the emergency room where they immediately fitted me with a stiff collar to stabilize my head and neck.

Afterward I went to my office, feeling like I had just been thrown off a cliff. I briefly met with my three partners to tell them what the scan had shown. I would be out of work . . . indefinitely.

Over my many years as a practicing lung specialist, I sat across from countless patients with similar news: "I'm sorry, your tests show that you have lung cancer." In every case, I watched the expression of doom come upon their faces and those of their loved ones.

Until now, I had never experienced the fear and shock those cancer victims endured. But now I was one in the same fraternity.

As I walked to my office, my mind filled with dark thoughts of what my future looked like. How long did I have to live? The tumor location could quite possibly compress the spinal cord in my neck. Would I spend the rest of my days as a quadriplegic? What would be my level of pain and suffering?

As a relatively new believer in Christ, I knew in the back of my mind that I should pray and trust God here. But I was in such a state of shock, I was unable to pray.

In his book, *The Bend in the Road*, author and pastor Dr. David Jeremiah related the terror he faced when diagnosed with lymphoma, a cancer of the lymph glands. He used the term *"disruptive moments"*, coined by author Gordon MacDonald, to describe unwelcome events that God allows in our lives, such as a cancer diagnosis. Dr. Jeremiah described his own diagnosis like this:

It was a profoundly disruptive moment in my life. This was no bump in the road; it was a gigantic . . . pothole. Life is difficult and difficulty is the only path to wisdom.

For certain, I had hit a gigantic "pothole" in my own life, my "disruptive moment." But what I was not yet able to process was how it could be a path to wisdom.

At that point, the only thing going through my mind was how I was going to give my wife this bad news.

Cooka and I were supposed to be celebrating our thirty-second wedding anniversary that night by going to a dinner theater at Regent University in Virginia Beach. I had to call home and tell her that we would not be able to go and that I would be home shortly to explain. I drove home that Friday night with the scan image of the tumor burning in my brain; I can still see that picture now as I write this. I was dreading having to share the ugly news of what was happening, having to see the look of doom which would surely register on her face.

When I arrived home, I sat Cooka down on the sofa and I told her what had happened earlier in the day. "It's not what we thought it was," I said. My discomfort wasn't what we thought during all these months of pain and suffering but was instead a tumor. What I remember is that she was strong and supportive, that we talked about what would happen next. I think she prayed for us as we sat together on the sofa. We knew the next difficult feat was to call our children, Travis and Ashley, that night.

Dr. Griffith scheduled more MRI films and a needle biopsy of the mass for the beginning of the week.

As Murphy's Law would have it, the pathologist who was the best in the hospital on bone marrow cancers, my friend, Dr. John Maddox, was on vacation and the other pathologists could not be certain what type of cells they were observing under the microscope. A repeat biopsy was done the following Monday.

When Dr. Maddox returned, he examined the material from the second biopsy and determined that the cells were plasma cells and that we were looking at a plasmacytoma. This diagnosis was a relief—because I knew this was not widespread cancer.

The next day I saw my good friend and oncologist, John Kessler, MD, who did a bone marrow biopsy in his office.

I still remember how upbeat he was, saying "Shaw-man, we are going to cure this. This has a ninety percent chance of cure with radiation."

Cooka and I were buoyed greatly by the report and thanked God for this diagnosis and good prognosis. What we did not yet realize was that this positive statistic was for local "cure" in the bone involved. But most people went on years later to develop full blown multiple myeloma (plasma cell cancer of the bone marrow) involving many bones throughout the body.

We wanted a second opinion regarding treatment options, so Dr. Kessler arranged an appointment for us at the Mayo Clinic with Martha Lacy, MD, a member of the world class department studying multiple myeloma.

It was extremely painful flying and changing planes with the neck discomfort, weak C7 vertebral body, and a stiff collar. Any movement or wobble of my neck caused shooting pains in my back near the left shoulder blade.

Although the "Big Clinic" experience at Mayo was a bit overwhelming, Dr. Lacy was very compassionate, explaining and responding to my questions patiently. She confirmed the diagnosis and agreed with radiation treatment.

The Mayo trip was very reassuring and we felt God was leading us. On August 3, I began radiation treatments under Dr. Wasserman my radiation oncologist. After about a week of treatments, I was able to return to my office, seeing a few patients each day, still wearing my stiff collar.

Spiritually, this time was very tough for me. Although I felt blessed to not have metastatic cancer, I was in pain and emotionally shell-shocked. I had difficulty praying or even concentrating on God. I could not come up with much more than *please heal me, Lord*" in my prayers.

Fortunately, God again blessed me by keeping Cooka at my side during this and subsequent crises with myeloma. She went right to the Word of God and printed out many of God's passages on suffering and His promises to be with us through pain and suffering and to heal us. She plastered these verses all over the house—words of hope and healing were taped to our refrigerator, bedside tables, bathroom mirrors and desktops.

Everywhere I looked, I had God's Word reminding me, "Yes, I am with you . . . you are not alone." Since I had much difficulty praying, Cooka did most of "our" praying for us and solicited all of our wonderful, Williamsburg Community Chapel friends to pray for me as well. She kept me lifted up when I wanted to be down and kept me from thinking negatively when I couldn't see the positive.

Other than my faith, Cooka is my greatest gift from God. This bout with cancer was the second major event God used to grow our marriage closer into "oneness"- the first event being three-and-a-half years earlier when I accepted Christ as my Lord and Savior.

I wonder how I could have ever made it through this crisis without faith in Jesus and my partner-in-faith, Cooka. Additionally, the support of my Christian friends was then, and continues to be, very significant. This includes my men's small group, our couples' small group, and other close friends in Christ at the Williamsburg Community Chapel, our home church. I believe that our all-knowing God was preparing me for this cancer when He brought me the faith in 1993. He knew that to make it through this crisis, it would be essential to hold on to my faith in Him and rely on the great support structure of my friends in Christ.

After my initial diagnosis, I shared the news with my pastor at that time, Bill Warrick, with whom I met regularly on Thursday afternoons. He drove me to a meeting of our church elders so they could pray over and anoint me with oil for healing as James 5:14 promises:

Is anyone among you sick? Let him call for the elders of the church, and let them pray over him, anointing him with oil in the name of the Lord. And the prayer of faith will save the sick, and the Lord will raise him up.

I was quite uplifted by the prayers and laying on of hands by the elders. God was gathering and rallying support for the coming storm, which would prove even worse.

Four weeks into my radiation therapy, the pain in my neck and shoulder worsened rather than improved. It was so severe that I could not sit or stand with my neck in a full upright position. I could only gain some relief by tilting my head to the right. I arranged a cervical spine x-ray and was shocked to find that C7 now looked partially collapsed on the left. The radiation had damaged the remaining bone and it had buckled beneath the weight of my head like a crushed egg shell, despite the support of the stiff collar.

Not only did the MRI confirm this, but it also suggested something wrong with an adjacent vertebral body *and* that I had spinal cord compression on the left. Dr. Griffith determined that I needed surgery and it would be done at the University of Virginia Medical Center (UVA) in Charlottesville. It was Labor Day weekend, and I waited three long days at home before I could schedule a surgery appointment. I was wracked with pain and unable to move my leg due to the spinal cord compression.

On Tuesday, Dr. Griffith called to let us know that we had an appointment for Wednesday with Dr. Shaffray, a neurosurgeon who specializes in cancer of the spine. Once again, we had been totally blindsided by test results. I had visions of becoming a paraplegic from cord injury or even dying from cancer that had been misdiagnosed as plasmacytoma. It seemed hopeless and dire, and I know there were times when I cried out to God, *"Where are you in all of this?"*

One of the most emotional moments during this part of my cancer story was when I spoke with my son, Travis, after I had learned about the vertebral collapse, cord compression and immediate need for surgery.

Travis was in Fredericksburg taking pre-med classes at Mary Washington College and working at the time. With all he had on his own plate, he called me with great concern to ask how I was doing. "I am just trying to stay alive right now, son," I said.

The fact that both of my kids expressed so much love and care during my various cancer crises still touches me today and makes me give thanks to the Lord, that He could give us such compassionate children.

On that Wednesday, our good friend, Jim McCulloch, drove us to Charlottesville to see the neurosurgeons. It was the first time I used a wheelchair in this ordeal, as my pain and leg weakness did not allow me to walk the long distance to the neurosurgery clinic. The neurosurgeon and his chief resident saw me and agreed that I needed surgery as soon as possible but he could not get operating room time until five days later.

They relayed the severity of the problem and stressed that it was possible that the disease was in an adjacent vertebral body. This could make the surgery very long—possibly up to ten to twelve hours. The risk of paralysis was real, as was the threat of a stroke—the tumor encased an artery supplying my brain on the left side.

All of this was of course very frightening to us. Cooka told me later that the neurosurgeons were ecstatic that they had such a challenging, complicated surgical case. (Unfortunately, I know that many docs have this feeling at times, not recognizing the suffering that their patient and family are undergoing.)

I was admitted to UVA Hospital and Cooka went back to get things settled in Williamsburg. She returned the next day and stayed with me in my hospital room day and night until two days before discharge. I had an extensive workup including an arteriogram to ensure that I was at a low risk of stroke, in case the surgeon had to tie off the artery surrounded by tumor during surgery. I was kept in the Neurosurgical ICU the night after the arteriogram, and although I slept very little, I was glad to have a good nurse and resident surgeon.

Cooka set up a twenty-four-hour prayer vigil with family and friends. With most of our family there in the waiting room, Pastors Bill Warrick and Tuck Knupp conducted a prayer service with singing and scripture reading while I was in surgery. Cooka said it was a moving and powerful spiritual experience, with the Presence of God evident in the room. My wonderful wife was even able to share my testimony of becoming a believer.

The only imperfect thing from this spiritual moment was that Travis missed it all—due to his having to take a test in one of his pre-med courses in Fredericksburg. I plan to ask God about that one in Heaven: *"Why, Lord, couldn't Travis be there to hear my faith story and be part of this wonderful moment?"*

God was clearly at work in my life but I still had difficulty praying and concentrating on my Bible reading due to the distraction of pain, the busy workup in the hospital and my raw fear and anxiety of anticipating the risky surgery. My beloved wife kept me covered in prayer, read Scripture and together we sang and played praise music on a portable CD player.

Even today, eighteen years later, I do not believe my surgery would have been as successful without the prayer support we had before, during, and after the procedure.

SURGERY AND THE POST-OP BATTLE

During the surgery, I remember being in an area that was, I thought, the pre-op holding area. In reality it was actually the operating room and I was under traction on a stretcher, fitted with my "halo" ring device immobilizing my neck. I think I was talking to an anesthesia resident and then everything went blank. The next thing I remember was blackness, hearing voices then looking up at fuzzy faces. I immediately asked for John Truitt MD, the head of the Pulmonary Division at the University of Virginia, who was a friend I had met at state lung meetings.

They assured me that I had no airway problems, that everything was fine. But I was frightened, convinced that these doctors did not know about medical airway issues (Yes, I know this was silly but post-op thoughts are not always rational.) I insisted that they call Dr. Truitt to come in and see me, even though he was in his car and halfway home. Demonstrating grace and kindness, Dr. Truitt turned his car around and came in, checked me out, and reassured me that everything was fine.

Immediately after surgery, my neurosurgeon rushed to the fifth floor waiting area and literally ran after Cooka as she walked to the elevator. He was so excited that he had finished in only five hours and was able to remove the cancerous C7 vertebral body and fuse C6 to T1 without any complications. This was a wonderful relief to Cooka, who was extremely anxious about the potential complications of prolonged, extensive surgery.

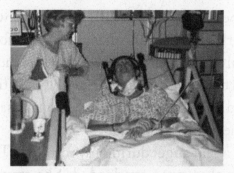

During this time, my survival depended more on Cooka's compassion and love than on my own. She has been a wonderful partner, nurse and caregiver throughout the nineteen year illness. I doubt I would have survived two transplants and fusion surgery without her loving care.

Throughout that first night in the Neurosurgical ICU, I had little confidence in the nursing staff and didn't sleep a wink. My controlling personality convinced me I had to stay awake to make sure the nurses and neurosurgery resident did not screw something up- as if I was in any position to detect a mistake or do anything about it. Surely, I was not in control.

The first post-op morning was interesting. On neurosurgery rounds around six in the morning, the orthopedic resident came in with the neurosurgery resident and roughly loosened the saddle part of the halo device at the split over my upper sternum. He jerked and pulled to open the plastic support in order to remove a drain in my lower neck. I felt like I was being torn apart, muscle and tissue from bone. "Stop, please!" I yelled, but he just kept going without paying much attention to me or how much it hurt.

A halo is a graphite and titanium device used to immobilize the neck so it can't move while the spine heals from surgery. Essentially, it's a sophisticated way of "splinting the neck" like an arm splinted after surgery on the bones. It is typically prescribed to be worn 24/7, usually for twelve weeks. My halo consisted of a ring attached to my skull with four sterile bolts to hold it firmly in place. The ring was attached by rods to a saddle-like part that fit over my head and was tightly strapped to my chest and back. Therefore the stationary saddle prevented my head and neck from moving.

Cooka was a real angel during my recovery. The nurses were very sweet, but they were overloaded. She stayed in my room twenty-four hours a day, providing me with the companionship and "nursing" assistance I needed. This was easy and natural for her as she has a very compassionate nature and years of previous experience as a registered nurse. I was in good hands.

Beyond her nursing experience, Cooka's years as a high school cheerleader also proved prophetic as she kept me going during this trial of cancer surgery. She was upbeat when I was depressed and optimistic when I was whiny and demanding. She encouraged me forcefully when I wanted to simply surrender to weakness and not walk the halls.

I was practically helpless due to post-op weakness in my left arm, hand and leg. Cooka played Christian music and read Scripture on and off during the day. She gave me baths and summoned the nurses when I needed them. She was THE major gift from God—other than His Presence and Support that enabled me to recover from the surgery, both in the hospital and at home.

Walking was one of the biggest challenges I faced during my recovery. I used a walker with the physical therapist at first, then with just Cooka. But it was tough—I had become severely de-conditioned from lack of exercise before surgery and muscle weakness caused by Decadron, a very high-potency steroid used to diminish swelling related to spinal cord compression. With work and determination, I was soon able to ambulate the halls with a walker and walk up at least three steps with a cane, a necessary criterion for discharge.

I also experienced swallowing difficulty caused by pre-op radiation which affected my esophagus, post-surgical effects, and a fungal infection in my throat after the operation.

The neurosurgeon was definitely not a warm, fuzzy physician and had little in the way of a bedside manner. However, it was clear that he knew what he was doing and had a great team of neurosurgery residents. I knew that our being at UVA was God's Provision and His Grace for me and I was grateful.

At last the day of discharge came, but the trip home was quite challenging. I was extremely weak and anxious about leaving the support and security of the hospital. Just getting dressed gave me such a rapid heart rate that Dr. Truitt gave me an electrocardiogram check before discharging me.

Our wonderful friends, the McCullochs, came up to drive me home in the spacious comfort of their Cadillac. We did not anticipate how difficult it would be for me to bend over enough to ease myself into the car with the extra weight and girth of the halo. We tried the back seat, but it quickly became apparent that was impossible. We have a picture of the discharge attendant barely squeezing me into the front seat. I was not prepared for the pain that minimal undulations in the pavement would cause in my neck and head—every slight movement registered in my skull where the halo bolts were attached. The ride home was VERY tense and painful, despite the luxury suspension of the Cadillac.

Upon arriving at the house, it took the McCullochs and Cooka to hoist me out of the car. Together, we negotiated the front steps, as I held tightly to my cane, glad to be free of the walker. I never used the walker again. I felt the joy of graduation—I had moved from inability to walking immediately post-op, to being free of all ambulatory assistance other than a cane.

A rented hospital bed had been set up in our bedroom. I settled into sleeping either on my right side or my left side, as the halo superstructure was square and sleeping on my back would cause sleep apnea with upper airway obstruction from my tongue. That left only side sleep positions.

Everything was an adjustment.

Cooka met my every need: nurse, cook, body washer—I wasn't able to shower for three months- and spiritual encourager. I had many ups and downs during my recovery, constant neck pain, and a weepy, sad disposition that required an antidepressant medication. But Cooka never let me give up.

As I grew stronger physically I began to feel my legs again, but I still had difficulty regaining my spiritual balance. Cooka helped me with Scripture reading and music, but I struggled to concentrate on God's Word due to my extreme physical discomfort. It felt as if my prayers were going nowhere, never really reaching God. I felt a degree of isolation and disconnect from Him which I had never felt before.

C.S. Lewis described similar thoughts in *A Grief Observed* when he was grieving over the death of his wife:

> **Meanwhile where is God . . . When you are happy . . . if you turn to Him with gratitude and praise, you will be welcomed with open arms. But go to Him when your need is desperate, when all other help is vain, and what do you find? A door slammed in your face, and a sound of bolting and double bolting on the inside. After that, silence.**

I never did stop praying; mostly for my recovery and healing from the surgery and radiation. I asked Pastor Bill Warrick if he could explain why I felt this isolation from God but he could give me no answer. In *My Utmost for His Highest*, Oswald Chambers speaks of the "Trial of Faith" where "faith being worked out into reality must experience times of unbroken isolation." I experienced this isolation in those days before and after my surgery; this was definitely my own "Trial of Faith."

The New Testament book of James 1:2-4 says of such trials:

My brethren, count it all joy when you fall into various trials, knowing that the testing of your faith produces patience. But let patience have its perfect work, that you may be perfect and complete, lacking nothing.

Despite the isolation and frustration I felt then, I can see now the growth and perseverance of my faith in Christ that occurred during those difficult times was huge. During my "halo" time, I was greatly inspired by several books: *Don't Waste Your Sorrows* by Paul Billheimer, *You Gotta Keep Dancin'* by Tim Hansel, and L.B. Cowman's *Streams in the Desert*. These three books encouraged me by stressing perseverance of faith in the face of pain and suffering. They reminded me to look forward to the growth of faith and character in each trial, to recognize that God knows what you are going through and walks with you in your pain. These were important messages.

I also meditated and memorized many passages of Scripture on suffering. Through these books, reading God's Word and prayer time, God revealed to me that He grows us the most spiritually and emotionally during times of trial; and I was experiencing a major league "growth spurt" thanks to my ordeal with cancer.

To my surprise, I became accustomed to the halo after about four weeks, and even learned how to sleep on my side, although it was often with the help of prescription drugs. I gradually settled into a "normal" daily routine; taking long walks with Cooka and our dachshund, futzing around the garage, and even blowing leaves into the woods with an electric blower.

We were sometimes able to slip into the back of church on Sundays and I attended the Friday Bible study breakfast on a few occasions. After eight to ten weeks, the halo seemed to become part of me. I was ambivalent as we approached twelfth week—I knew we'd be headed to UVA to have the halo removed, but I wasn't sure whether I would have joy or pain once it came off.

When that day came, I was reluctantly led into the narrow, dark procedure room, sweating profusely. I was dismayed when the neurosurgeon sent an intern in to remove the halo. *What? A baby-faced intern, less than twelve months out of medical school!* I was terrified when he placed a stiff collar on my neck and started to loosen the posts and saddle. At last, my neurosurgeon showed up to remove the bolts in my skull. What a strange feeling that was; not much pain at the bolt sites, but my neck was in agony as soon as the halo was removed. Without the support of the halo, my neck wobbled painfully. I didn't walk far before I wanted to go back and ask to have the halo re-applied.

The white stiff collar underneath the halo rods—immobilized my neck when the halo was finally removed.

My neck throbbed with pain for the next several weeks—without the support of the halo I had to rely on my neck muscles to hold up my head, but those muscles were severely atrophied due to lack of use. I was afraid to let friends hug me because each gesture of kindness and love bent my neck painfully. Still, I gritted my teeth and Cooka and I flew to Jackson Hole for Christmas with Travis, Ashley, and her husband. It was a tough trip, but I wouldn't have traded anything for the wonderful time we had together as a family, celebrating Christ's birthday.

Over the next year, I slowly regained my strength through physical therapy exercises at a local sports center. I gradually increased my workload at my practice, and even started taking some night calls. By the fall of 1998 I was taking one day of weekend call every three or four weeks. A full recovery seemed like a very real possibility.

There was still a cloud over my medical situation, however, as my blood M-protein level (measurement of myeloma activity) was slowly rising. This cloud rained down on me in the summer of 2001, when I developed a sharp pain in my left chest while working on a bicycle in the garage of our summer home in Idaho. I knew I probably had sustained a non-traumatic rib fracture, most likely secondary to the cancer. However, I just kept going until I returned to Williamsburg in August and x-rays showed a healing fourth rib fracture.

The pain reoccurred in October, with x-rays showing more rib destroyed; a rib biopsy confirmed plasmacytoma.

I underwent another course of radiation therapy, and left my practice again, this time presumably for good. One year later, I had recurrent pain in the same rib—x-rays showing that the 2001 rib radiation had missed the edge of the plasmacytoma. I had my third bout with what they now identified as multiple myeloma- which is the name for cancer when multiple, malignant, plasmacytomas are present in the bone marrow

My fourth bout with multiple myeloma in March 2003 was manifested by left hip pain and cancer in a pelvic bone. My M-protein level was now much higher at 2.5. "It's time to get the big guns out," said Dr. Kessler. This meant chemotherapy with high dose dexamethasone, a steroid shown to kill myeloma cells; and later, with thalidomide, an older drug that had been recently shown to be active against myeloma cancer. This was all in preparation for an autologous stem cell transplant (using my own stem cells) following high dose chemotherapy with melphalan to be done at MCV in their Bone Marrow Transplant Unit. Melphalan is a highly active chemotherapy agent against myeloma.

The high dose dexamethasone (Decadron) was very difficult to tolerate—it caused irritability, weakness, loss of muscle mass, and appetite suppression that resulted in weight loss that I didn't need. One of the most distressing side effects of dexamethasone for me was sleep deprivation—sleepless nights affected my memory and alertness during the day.

The autologous stem cell transplant proved to be an even more terrible ordeal. The procedure was designed to give me enough melphalan to wipe out all of my bone marrow cells. The effect was potentially lethal because the treatment removed all of my white blood cells, and without transplanted stem cells, I could not fight off infections.

Two days later, I underwent "stem cell rescue"—stem cells that had been collected from my blood three weeks earlier were infused into my intravenous lines. It took about seven days before my white blood cells, started from the stem cells, began producing and repopulated my bone marrow.

For two weeks I had severe diarrhea and nausea, both caused by melphalan damage to my gastrointestinal tract. A high fever and debilitating weakness added to all this misery during those weeks.

Fortunately, I had my son Travis (then in his final year at MCV med school) and Cooka to cheer me up. Even more important, I had Cooka and our believing friends holding me up before God with prayer. Just as the 'halo' period was a time of growth, this episode of post-transplant recovery became a time of surrender to God and growth in my faith.

When I finally see God in Heaven, I would also like to ask why He allowed so many traumatic events to occur during 2003. During the stem cell transplant season my mom had a heart attack, went into shock and respiratory failure, and died on September 3, just three weeks before my transplant.

On December 10, as I was just beginning to recover from a post-transplant colon infection, Travis was admitted to the hospital with severe, life-threatening pneumonia. Two days later Travis was placed on a ventilator for life support. Thankfully, our daughter Ashley, flew in from Wyoming for the extra support we needed at the time.

I prayed—and kept praying—to the Lord Jesus during my transplant ordeal. But I never prayed as hard or as ceaselessly as when Travis was on the ventilator! I can still remember crying out to God as we drove to the hospital not knowing if Travis would live or die, *"Why Lord? I have served You faithfully with the Lackey Free Clinic! Why would you take my son from me?"*

I was in my post-transplant isolation phase when Travis became ill. I would not, however, let this keep me from visiting him when he was in the ICU. No one was going to keep me out when my son was so near death. We were able to see Travis before he was sedated to go on the ventilator—I held his hand and told him not to worry, that we would be praying for him. I also told him I would dance in his ICU room when he came off the machine. Four days later, the breathing tube was removed, and I, fully gowned and masked for my protection, danced a 'jig' as I walked into the ICU room and saw him sitting up in bed and talking. He was discharged two days later.

The three of us stayed in Richmond at my mom's house while Travis recovered. This was a very tender and close time for all three of us, and we were grateful that God gave us the opportunity to serve Travis and watch him recover from a near-fatal illness.

Regardless of my own physical pain and challenges, my son's illness was undoubtedly the most stressful episode of the whole transplant ordeal. Here I was, a pulmonary/critical care doctor, expertly trained to treat life-threatening pneumonia. But because of my post-transplant isolation status, I was helpless and could do no more than watch and trust God that He would provide the physician and hospital that would allow Travis to survive.

As the Apostle Paul says in 2 Corinthians 9:15, "Thanks be to God for his indescribable gift" that He answered our prayers, granting us Travis' survival and full recovery.

My recovery from transplant was prolonged and painful due to a colon infection caused by an opportunistic bacterial agent that attacks patients after prolonged antibiotic usage. Although tests to detect this organism were negative at MCV, they were inexplicably, and correctly, positive at my Newport News gastroenterologist's lab a short time later. The delay in diagnosis resulted in persistent nausea, diarrhea, and loss of appetite. I could not ingest adequate food and lost thirty-nine pounds from my already slim body.

At that point in my cancer journey, I was a "baby" Christian, having come to faith only three-and-a-half years earlier. My story of faith was yet in its early chapters and I was still trying to find out what it really meant to follow Christ. What an introduction I had been given!

Fortunately in December 2003, the colon infection was finally treated successfully. I was able to resume a normal diet and began to gain weight. I once again started an exercise regimen to strengthen my atrophied muscles. I was soon started on the chemotherapeutic drug thalidomide to make the transplant induced remission last longer.

After a one-year course of this drug, I was blessed with almost six years of complete remission. I had no symptoms of myeloma, and my blood tests and scans showed no evidence of advancing cancer. I returned to normal activity—serving as Medical Director for the Lackey Free Clinic, exercising at the gym, riding my bicycle and playing golf.

In spite of advances in stem cell transplantation and the discovery of several new chemotherapeutic agents for treating multiple myeloma, this cancer remains incurable. As a physician,

I knew this and carried the possibility of relapse in my mind like a cloud throughout this period of "complete remission."

The cloud rained on me again in November 2009, when pain in my mid- and lower spine began to creep into my daily activities. Blood tests and MRIs confirmed re-occurance of myeloma; this time in my spine. "So what does this mean for prognosis?" I asked my oncologist, Dr. Kessler.

"Shaw-man, I think we can control this new disease," he answered. "We'll irradiate the involved vertebrae, and then put you on a chemotherapeutic regimen using the new highly active drugs just approved for myeloma."

My spirit was instantly buoyed by his optimistic outlook.

In March 2010, after taking time to recover from the four week course of radiation therapy to my spine, I started on what was the first of four chemotherapeutic regimens that would continue through April 2013. With each drug combination, I was able to obtain a partial remission of the myeloma. The remissions however, were not maintained and I would invariably have to move to the next regimen.

In November 2012, a PET scan ordered by Dr. Lacy at the Mayo Clinic revealed that the myeloma had spread to my liver. This finding, a poor prognostic sign, rekindled fearful memories of my 1997 MRI that first showed cancer in my neck.

Dr. Lacy's suggestion for treatment was to consider a second stem cell transplant. She told us that the Mayo Clinic team had had some good responses using a second transplant in myeloma relapses. But the stem cell transplant is a rigorous process, which brings with it significant pain and suffering. And, at nearly seventy years of age, I was at increased risk of complications. Hence, Cooka and I spent much time in prayer, asking God for His Will in going forward with this transplant.

Through our prayers and those of our Christian friends, we felt led by the Holy Spirit to proceed despite the risks. I was admitted to MCV for a second transplant on May 21, 2013.

The Unit

"Lord, I thank you for giving me the privilege of access to this mode of treatment in this excellent unit. You have blessed me with many believing nurses." ~ From my journal, June 1, 2013

"Good morning, Dr. Shaw—welcome to the Bone Marrow Transplant Unit."

Although the oncologist head of the unit was pessimistic and did not believe that another transplant would achieve remission from the bone marrow cancer I had been fighting for seventeen years, I remained optimistic.

It was May 2013 and here I was, making my second visit to the BMTU in ten years. I'd gone through the sequential failure of four chemotherapy regimens since 2010.

Much like the first visit, this second event has been seared into my memory bank like no other; the sounds, the sights and the smells are as real to me today as they were then.

Many things on the unit had improved due to a remodel five years earlier. This time, I could see that an attempt had been made to make the unit more visually attractive to patients suffering the dark reality of cancer. There were pale sky blue and yellow walls instead of the drab light brown found in 2003. The hallways were decorated with colorful art created and donated by former patients, as well as framed, short phrases urging perseverance, survival, and dependence on God.

I walked these halls daily to fight the deconditioning of chemotherapy. The visual reality of cancer appeared repeatedly on those walks—a room with a toddler, his mother sitting beside him reading a magazine; an 11-year-old boy without any hair watching cartoons; a middle-aged woman and an elderly man, always in bed, too weak to take the same slow laps that I made.

Curiosity kept jabbing me to find out who was in the room I'd had for the first transplant. The door was usually closed—indicating that there was a very sick patient in there. Finally, after a week of walks, I saw her: a middle aged woman connected to two intravenous bags (like me) but with her bed rails up during the day—a bad sign, one that probably meant she was not doing well.

Hospital odors can be difficult to describe. Unlike some parts of the hospital, the transplant unit smelled fresh and pleasant. The director was necessarily compulsive about cleanliness in order to protect the unit's immunocompromised patients from exposure to environmental germs. But there was one smell that jolted everyone's olfactory system—rotten eggs. The rotten egg odor appeared only when someone was receiving his transplant stem cells. The cells were frozen in a liquid agent similar to hydrogen sulfide—the odiferous agent in spoiled eggs. As the intravenous line drips in stem cells suspended in this agent, the patient smells like a large basket of rotten eggs baked in the sun. The door is kept closed as the smell can travel all the way to the end of the hall. The oppressive smell sometimes forced spouses and family members to spend less bedside time for up to twenty-four hours following the infusion.

My dedicated wife never left my side.

Hospitals are supposed to be quiet zones, but my personal experience as both a treating physician and as a patient has taught me that hospital hallways are much too noisy for a patient's rest and peace. The BMTU, however, was an exception. The hallway was noisy only when the medical team made its daily rounds.

Like most patients, I did not mind the noise. I knew the sound of the team coming down the hall meant that I would soon be hearing the report on my condition, particularly the status of my blood cell counts indicating the 'take' of my transplanted stem cells. Quiet resumed in the hallway once the medical team had finished its rounds.

A much bigger sound problem happened during the normal hours of sleep, when I was bombarded with various high pitched alarms from the electronic devices used to infuse different fluids and monitor patient vital signs. These alarm reminded me of trying to sleep in a game arcade filled with eleven-year-olds. Of course, the alarm called a nurse to repeat vital signs or reset the intravenous pump. Sleep deprivation is the mantra of the day (and night). As the days in the Unit piled up, my accumulated sleep deficit began to feel like being on the bottom of a goal line pileup with the whole Redskin defensive line on top of me.

In spite of these sometimes troublesome sensory assaults, the BMTU remains a place of life and hope for me- life and hope for patients who have exhausted all other modes of cancer treatment, life and hope for family members and loved ones, life and hope to hold the next grandchild. As for me, life and hope blessed me to follow Christ's mandate to serve "the least of these" in our community.

Life on a transplant ward. I'm taking an exercise stroll on the transplant unit with my brother, Chris.

No Remission, No Immunity

"You will not fear ... the pestilence that stalks in the darkness, nor the plague that destroys at midday." ~ Ps. 91:6

"It looks like we didn't get remission of the myeloma with this second transplant," he said. "I'm sorry."

This news from the transplant physician was like a punch to my solar plexus—I couldn't take a breath for many seconds. He mentioned the possibility of a research study with a new agent in the drug pipeline. But, I barely heard him . . . I was not yet interested in a drug study.

The following day, I called my trusted Mayo Clinic expert, Dr. Martha Lacy, and relayed the details of the transplant results.

Next, I met with Dr. Kessler, my local oncologist, and discussed remaining treatment options. After conversation between Dr. Lacy and Dr. Kessler, they recommended we pluck the last apple off the chemotherapy tree, a brand new anti-myeloma drug that my cancer had not yet been exposed to, hence it should not be resistant to: the drug, pomalidomide.

On February 1, 2014, I started on oral pomalidomide (Pomalyst) daily and dexamethasone, once weekly by mouth.

Over the ensuing ten months, this new regimen proved effective according to blood tests followed to monitor myeloma cancer activity. However, the recent autologous transplant, chemotherapy, and the notable impaired immunity associated with myeloma all combined to put me in an immunocompromised state for all of 2014. The impaired immunity was like a large hammer hovering over Cooka's and my travel opportunities and our participation in social activities.

Ultimately, the hammer fell on us several times in that year: pneumonia, which required a five day hospitalization in March, a parasitic infection of my intestines in August requiring a five day hospitalization, and bronchitis and sinusitis in November that required two courses of antibiotics.

Even now—lastly, most significantly, I am writing today at home recovering from a life-threatening pneumonia, complicated by kidney failure. I was hospitalized at Medical College of Virginia for nearly four weeks. During part of that time, I was on life support with a ventilator and dialysis machine. My doctors were concerned that I would not survive this infection. Praise the Lord that my son Travis, who is now also a physician, my devoted wife, and my daughter were at my side throughout the dangerous phases of the illness.

There was much prayer offered during this time. I was too ill, and often too disoriented, to pray myself. But Cooka, our church family, and our Lackey Free Clinic family pummeled Heaven with prayers during the entire hospitalization.

I was never alone.

God was surely with me every step of this illness. It was His Pleasure and His healing grace that allowed me to survive.

This is just the most recent episode of God protecting me from potentially lethal circumstances over the course of my lifetime. Divine Intervention has seen me through an auto accident, a serious college football injury, hypothermia in the Long Island Sound following a boating accident, spinal cord surgery, stem cell transplants, and three episodes of pneumonia since 2013, including the most recent severe episode of January 2015.

It has become obvious to my family and friends that **life has become ever so meaningful to me.** What life I have left will be spent honoring God and helping the world around me see Him and appreciate the life we were given.

A paragraph from A.B. Simpson in the devotional book *Streams in the Desert* says it best:

The pressure of hard places makes us value life. Every time our life is given back to us from such a trial, it is like a new beginning, and we learn better each time how much it is worth, and hopefully make more of it for God and man. The pressure helps us to understand the trials of others, and fits us to help and sympathize with them.

The Middle or Third Rail: The Power of God

"... I tell you the truth, whatever you do for one of the least of these brothers of mine, you did for me." ~ Matt. 25:40

Cooka and I have often been complimented on the wonderful vision *we* have had for Lackey, but this is just not true. The only vision we had was to go to Rising Sun Baptist Church on Thursday nights and see whichever patients came through the door. We had no vision beyond that. Our only vision was to follow Him, go through the doors He opened for us, and make sure that all the ministry moves that we made were centered on serving Jesus by loving the poor and disadvantaged that came through the clinic doors. A verse we often refer to in this situation is from the Gospel of Luke:

"So you also, when you have done everything you were told to do, should say, 'We are unworthy servants; we have only done our duty.'" ~ Luke 17:10

Throughout this season, what has happened to us spiritually? Well, this is where we find **the middle rail of the train track**.

During this time battling cancer, we were driven deeper into God's Word and prayer. Cooka placed scripture verses all over the house: on the mirrors, on the ice box, and on the bedside tables. I meditated on multiple verses to battle pain and suffering.

For example, Isaiah 43:1-2 says:

> **Do not fear, for I have redeemed you; I have summoned you by name; you are mine. When you pass through the waters I will be with you; and when you pass through the rivers they will not sweep over you. When you walk through the fire, you will not be burned . . .**

And Psalm 41:1-3, which really spoke to me:

> **Blessed is he who has regard for the weak. The Lord delivers him in times of trouble. The Lord will protect him and save his life . . . The Lord will sustain him on his sickbed, and restore him from his bed of illness.**

These were the promises that I claimed during this period by digging deeper into God's Word. Like Job, we were trying to keep trusting God in the face of suffering:

> *"Though he slay me, yet will I trust in Him"* (Job 13:15).

I remember that at one point, Cooka was reading Isaiah 38, where Hezekiah got a promise from God to let him live another fifteen years (38:5). My wife claimed that verse for me . . . for us!

I just passed eighteen years post-diagnosis!

We were discouraged from building our own Clinic structure by the people at the state organizations, "You can't raise the money. It's too difficult. Nobody does this in a free clinic community." Cooka said, *"But, God!"*

And, in 2001, 2002, and 2003, when I experienced the three subsequent recurrences and relapses of the cancer, each requiring a course of radiation treatment, we continued to stand on God's Word.

We have had the mighty blessing of watching God work miracles- growing the ministry from three volunteers in a church Sunday school room with a cardboard box of medicine and supplies and so few patients that we considered closing several times, to our current facility of 10,000 square feet with a pharmacy and cutting-edge equipment, now including cardiac echocardiography and ultrasound labs.

Where we were once seeing fewer than one-hundred patients in the church, we are now seeing over 12,000 patient visits per year in a beautiful, $1.6 million facility, debt-free and funded entirely by donations. Again, Cooka said, *"But, God!"*

Just like the middle rail on that Lionel Train track provides the power to make things happen, it is His work that made this happen!

We thank God for his healing and comforting grace for us as He has helped me endure five courses of chemotherapy and radiation therapy, and two stem cell transplantations and allowed me to live twice the average survival time for this disease. With this extra time and period of remission, He has given me the privilege of working with awesome colleagues and following His vision to expand and grow the Lackey ministry.

What has God taught me through these experiences with cancer and the free clinic ministry?

Firstly, Romans 5:3-4 says:

"We also rejoice in our sufferings because we know that suffering produces perseverance; perseverance, character; and character, hope."

If God gives you a calling to serve Him, don't try to predict where He's going to lead you. Follow and persevere as He opens doors and works miracles. Trust and persevere through barriers that are thrown up along the way, as they were to us. More often than not this is spiritual warfare, where the evil one has raised up discouragement, like he did for us, through obstacles like planning departments, VDOT planners, fundraising obstacles, and state associations.

The evil one uses these in an attempt to distract you. We have learned to stay focused on Jesus, to stay focused on the vision that He has given us… Realize that, **"He who is in us is greater than he who is in the world."** (1 John 4:4).

Secondly, John 15:1-2 says:

"I am the true vine and my Father is the gardener. He cuts off every branch in me that bears no fruit, while every branch that bears fruit He prunes so it will be even more fruitful."

In Psalm 23:2, you may have to listen to hear the emphasis in the phrase:

"He <u>makes</u> me lie down in green pastures . . ." (emphasis on 'makes' is mine)

God made me lie down and pruned me from a busy pulmonary practice where I probably would have kept working had I not contracted myeloma. As a result, I feel He was leading me into a situation where, with remissions and treatments, I could shepherd and help the clinic get onto its feet so people like Medical Director Ralph Robertson, MD, and Executive Director Carol Sale, RN, could take over the leadership.

It took me several years to realize that my suffering with myeloma was God's pruning process for my life.

Philip Yancey, in *Where is God When it Hurts,* has a hopeful answer to the question of suffering when God prunes us. My pain **"holds out hope for the future, that even suffering can be transformed and 'redeemed'. A human tragedy . . . can be used to display God's work."**

To Cooka and me, being "pulled" out of my pulmonary practice by the pain and suffering of myeloma has been redeemed by the display of God's Power in the development of Lackey Free Clinic.

Thirdly, James 1:1-4 says:

> **"Consider it pure joy, my brothers and sisters, whenever you face trials of many kinds, because you know that the testing of your faith produces perseverance. Let perseverance finish its work so that you may be mature and complete, not lacking anything."**

God will allow pain and suffering to drive you deeper into your relationship with Him and mature you as a believer. It is no doubt this happened to me. It started right with the halo and has continued through the chemotherapy and the two stem cell transplants. I had no choice but to grow closer to God and to mature as a believer, and that was an important point for me.

As a result of my experiences, I prepared pamphlets many years ago, compiling "Scriptures for Comfort in Suffering," which you will find in the **appendix.** I have passed them out to my patients over the past several years when they have been in times of trial. If you haven't been through a trial—you will at some point in the future. Based on my experience, you will need God's Word for perseverance.

And last, but definitely not least, Psalm 32:6 says:

"Therefore, let everyone who is godly pray to you, while you may be found . . . you will protect me from trouble and surround me with songs of deliverance."

Prayer is critical in fighting health issues and in the development of a ministry. But, as it was for me at times, the prayer burden may have to be carried by others. As I found it difficult to pray during times of extreme pain such as the halo and the stem cell transplants, I had a wonderful life partner of fifty years in Cooka, who has been a saint in caring not only for my physical and emotional needs, but also in carrying the burden of prayer for us as a couple during these tough times.

We also benefitted tremendously from our small groups and our church family and, as I said earlier, even prayer groups from other churches that shouldered the prayer burden.

Today I feel blessed that I have been able to ride God's train as He has made His power available and visible to me. He built the Lackey ministry and allowed me to survive cancer longer than predicted so that I could serve Him by serving "the least of these."

Whenever somebody at the clinic exclaims, "Look at this miracle that God has done for us," I call on Paul's prayer for the Ephesian church, a prayer of exultation for the "power of the third rail," the immense authority of the Lord:

Now to Him who is able to do immeasurably more than all we ask or imagine, according to His power that is at work within us, to Him be glory in the church and in Christ Jesus throughout all generations, forever and ever! Amen. ~ Eph. 3:20-21

ABOUT THE AUTHOR

Dr. Jim Shaw, M.D., was a loving husband who celebrated fifty years of marriage with his wife and helpmate in life.

He was also the proud father of two adult children and three grandchildren.

From Williamsburg, Va., Dr. Shaw was a member and former elder at Williamsburg Community Chapel. He graduated from VCU School of Medicine, and trained in pulmonary medicine at Yale University and University of California San Diego. He was the Assistant Clinical Professor of Medicine at the Eastern Virginia Medical School in Norfolk, as well as the co-founder of the Lackey Free Clinic, along with his wife.

Holding various certifications, including one with the American Board of Internal Medicine as well as the Subspecialty Board of Pulmonary Disease, Dr. Shaw held memberships and positions in numerous, prestigious medical organizations.

Above all, however, it was his faith in Jesus Christ and service to the poor that is his greatest testimony.

APPENDIX

Scriptures for Comfort during Trials

Promise of Suffering

Psalm 23:2

He makes me lie down in green pastures.

1 Peter 4:12-13

Beloved, do not be surprised at the fiery ordeal that is taking place among you to test you, as though something strange were happening to you. But rejoice insofar as you are sharing Christ's sufferings, so that you may also be glad and shout for joy when His glory is revealed.

Purpose of Suffering

2 Corinthians 4:16-18

So we do not lose heart. Even though our outer nature is wasting away, our inner nature is being renewed day by day. For this slight momentary affliction is preparing us for an eternal weight of glory beyond all measure, because we look not at what can be seen but at what cannot be seen; for what can be seen is temporary, but what cannot be seen is eternal.

James 1:2-4

My brothers and sisters, whenever you face trials of any kind, consider it nothing but joy, because you know that the testing of your faith produces endurance; and let endurance have its full effect, so that you may be mature and complete, lacking in nothing.

Provision for Suffering

Psalm 41:1-3

Blessed are those who consider the poor; the LORD delivers them in the day of trouble. The LORD protects them and keeps them alive; they are called happy in the land. You do not give them up to the will of their enemies. The LORD sustains them on their sickbed; in their illness You heal all their infirmities.

Isaiah 41:10

So do not fear, for I am with you; do not be dismayed, for I am your God. I will strengthen you and help you; I will uphold you with My righteous right hand.

Isaiah 43:1-3

Do not fear, for I have redeemed you; I have called you by name, you are Mine. When you pass through the waters, I will be with you; and through the rivers, they shall not overwhelm you; when you walk through fire you shall not be burned, and the flame shall not consume you. For I am the LORD your God, the Holy One of Israel, your Savior.

Deuteronomy 33:27

The eternal God is your refuge, and underneath are the everlasting arms.

Psalm 23

Psalm 91

Job 13:15

Though He slay me, yet will I trust in Him.

<u>Reward for Suffering</u>

Psalm 40:2

He drew me up from the desolate pit, out of the miry bog, and set my feet upon a rock, making my steps secure.

Psalm 116:1-9

I love the LORD, because He has heard my voice and my supplications. Because He inclined His ear to me, therefore I will call on Him as long as I live. The snares of death encompassed me; the pangs of Sheol laid hold on me; I suffered distress and anguish.

Then I called on the name of the LORD: "O LORD, I pray, save my life!" Gracious is the LORD, and righteous; our God is merciful.

The LORD protects the simple; when I was brought low, He saved me. Return, O my soul, to your rest, for the LORD has dealt bountifully with you.

For you have delivered my soul from death, my eyes from tears, my feet from stumbling. I walk before the LORD in the land of the living.

Lamentations 3:22-22

The steadfast love of the LORD never ceases, His mercies never come to an end; they are new every morning; great is Your faithfulness.

Job 19:25-26

For I know that my Redeemer lives, and that at the last He will stand upon the earth. And after my skin has been destroyed, yet in my flesh I will see God.

BIBLIOGRAPHY

Billheimer, Paul. *Don't Waste Your Sorrows*. Fort Washington: CLC Publications, 1993.

Chambers, Oswald. *My Utmost for His Highest*. Grand Rapids: Discovery House Publishers, 1992.

Cowman, L.B. *Streams in the Desert*. Grand Rapids: Zondervan Publishing, 1997.

Hansel, Tim. *You Gotta Keep Dancin'*. Colorado Springs: David C. Cook, 1998.

Jeremiah, David. *A Bend in the Road*. Nashville: Thomas Nelson, 2002.

Lewis, C.S. *A Grief Observed*. San Francisco: Harper, 2009.

Lewis, C.S. *Mere Christianity*. San Francisco: Harper, 2009.

McDowell, Josh. *More than a Carpenter*. Carol Stream: Tyndale House Publishers, 1986.

Morrison, Frank. *Who Moved the Stone?*. London: Faber and Faber, 1975.

Yancey, Philip. *Where is God When it Hurts*. Grand Rapids: Zondervan Publishing, 1996.

THE LAST WORD

By "Cooka"

What woman doesn't enjoy having "the last word"? For me, my last word at this time is all about how blessed I feel to have spent the greatest part of my life being married to a man with the integrity and character of Jim Shaw. His tenacity and ability to stay focused no matter what was huge - and once he became a born again believer in Jesus Christ, there was no stopping him!

I called him by many names: Shawnee, Boyfriend, my "Ever Ready" bunny & my HULK... and I likened the cancer battle of over 18 + years as our ongoing "whack-a-mole" game. There were so many times when we thought he was starring death in the face, but he would rally back with full force ready to squeeze whatever life he could out of any situation. His stamina and determination was proven clear up to his last breath!

Even in January when he had to be transported via helicopter to MCV while on a ventilator, I thought it was our final good bye. Thankfully that was not the case! During those few weeks in critical care I had reminded Jim that 2015 was a very important year for us with two major events on the calendar. April would mark the 20th Anniversary of the founding of Lackey Free

Clinic and July would mark our 50th Wedding Anniversary. Despite taking a nasty fall on our aggregate driveway one week before the Clinic Gala, he not only was able to attend, but we even danced together! Three months later we found ourselves at Two Rivers Country Club celebrating our 50th Anniversary together with friends. He had made both events and two weeks later he slipped out of my arms and into the arms of Jesus! What a man of God! What a husband! What a father! What a doctor! What a friend!

Thank you Lord for giving him to us for 71 precious years!

MEMORABLE PHOTOS

Hunting in Canada – 1990

Whitewater tour down The Grand Canyon
1994

Golfing – Jim made a hole in one!
April 1995

Fly-fishing in Jackson Hole, Wyoming - 2001

Bicycle riding at Slick Rock, Moab Utah – 2002

Happy Birthday Shawnee! – A new kayak
April 2003

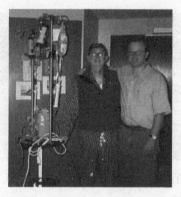

Walking the halls with son Travis after the first
stem cell transplant - September 2003

Recovered and ready to ride!
June 2004

Jim and daughter Ashley – 2012

Jan 4, 2015 – Airlifted to MCV

Home after another brush with death – Jan 23, 2015

Jim and Cooka dancing at the Lackey Clinic Gala
April 2015

Celebrating our 50th Wedding Anniversary
July 12, 2015

Jim's license plate
"Each of you should use whatever gift you have
received to serve others, as faithful stewards
of God's grace in its various forms."

To learn more about Lackey Clinic,
keep up with current events,
find opportunities to serve or to make a donation:
Visit our website
www.lackeyclinic.org

Printed in the United States
By Bookmasters